MW01632236

PRESUMED

JEWISH

Frontispiece
Charles Wehrenberg in Aspen 1967
photograph by Ed Bear

pages 6-130
Travelogue, photographs and notebook drawings
by Charles Wehrenberg 1972

page 125
1968 KMPX SuperBall Poster
photograph by Tom Wier

pages 130-141
Sally Larsen: *WTC Aftermath 2001*
photographs, paintings and prints by Sally Larsen

page 83
Yellow '72 VW Squareback
watercolor by Don Moses ~1978

pages 142-143
Sally Larsen ***OROTONES:***
Chambers Fine Art, NYC, September 2001;
NYC installation photographs by Ira Nowinski

SZP flip-book design by Charles Wehrenberg
cover photographs & collage by Sally Larsen
rear cover *Turkey,Persia* map; J. Wells/McNally 1866

ISBN 978 1-886163-93-5
first POD edition

A Puff now...a Puff then
my go-to Middle Eastern & Indian music CDs
see page 90

PRESUMED JEWISH

A DRIVE THROUGH THE MIDDLE EAST

Charles Wehrenberg

Solo Zone
San Francisco

otherwise

by Charles Wehrenberg

The Money Tree a grow book offered as $1000 hand-typed copies only -- 1968

Games of Competitive Relaxation bio-input table game: *Will Ball* -- 1973/75

Deep Relaxation, the Meditative Control of Smoking & Overeating LP -- 1975

Channel 1 Mood Synthesizer booklet -- *1980*

Channel 1 Mood Synthesizer patent -- *1982*

Round Bottom Volumetric patent -- *1982*

A Private Passion fine art article *UNITED Inflight Magazine* -- April 1984

Will Ball, the Game of Competitive Relaxation, software for Apple II -- 1984

An Interactive Novelist's Wish List article *New Media Magazine* -- Feb 1993

Will Ball sci-fi novel -- SZP 1995

Before New York historical novel -- SZP 1995

The Ploy of Cooking novel -- SZP 1995

Radio-Reactive Apples stories -- SZP 1995

Thrasher [illegible] -- SZP 1998

Fengshui graphic novel -- SZP 1998

Mississippi Blue photography monograph -- Twin Palms 2002

Movies Worth Watching More Than Once viewing guide -- SZP 2005

How To Survive Your Mouth lifestyle -- SZP ebook 2010

for
my fellow
seekers
ON THE
ROAD

Nikon

Presumed Jewish

September 2001

The murder of the World Trade Center in New York City conjured all manner of demons. Once again ancient rhetoric had flared with great violence. Once again there would be a violent reaction. Obviously, self-righteousness continues to stalk civilization. As inner voices chattered, wraiths swirled from the dust of my own encounter with the Middle East. I shuffled through old notebooks and color slides; I still felt blocked. What was I not seeing? Could I write my way to it? I told myself I should try, aware that the effort would require my questioning the naive innocence which continues to haunt my beliefs. Which is to say our belief in the right of others to believe as they may.

So, I set out to reflect on my 1971/72 road trip to India by way of Afghanistan. Little did I know in 2002 that the key I sought then would elude me for yet another 20 years! The title *Presumed Jewish* came in a glib moment along the way. Finally, a 16th-century fatwā from Timbuktu opened the doors of perception; it came to me with the COVID pandemic of 2020!

My drive about the Islamic diaspora began as a rug-to-riches fantasy 50 years ago after I bought a rare Persian carpet in London! The brilliant graphic work of MC Escher had revealed the power of Islamic design; I wanted to learn more about that. One thing was leading to another in the wake of *The Teachings of Don*

Juan, back when the truth was to be found *On the Road*...if you are listening. Oh really? One finds allies by listening! Is there more to know? Let's Go! Simple as that.

Taking a quick step back: after a mad-cap road trip from Aspen to San Francisco in a magic bus that I put together for a ride, 1967/69 were a strobe light of fast custom motorcycles, strong LSD, Acapulco Gold, Panama Red, underground FM radio, ballroom concerts, posters, underground comix, and the Portola Institute (birthplace of *The Whole Earth Catalog*), not to mention endless bottles of Taittinger Champagne and Cordon Blue cognac.

In late '67 I turned a wannabe garage operation in Berkeley into a thriving custom motorcycle business overnight with my connections to underground radio in San Francisco. This all came about because I had agreed to build the customized magic bus in Aspen which allowed New York DJ Ed Bear [see page 126/127] to come along for the ride. Once in San Francisco, we got a house together in Haight Ashbury and Bear took an on-air job with KMPX, the first underground FM radio station in San Francisco. Perceiving Ed Bear as an influencer, I set out to play with social media. I had done so before in 1963, using radio repartee in Indianapolis to promote my pop-up rock-n-roll dances.

Over the air, Bear put out the word about Mother's Motors. Customers came streaming in, wallets open wide. I knew they would! Bear was great on the air because he made people feel part of things by dropping celebrity into their hopes and dreams with such great ease. Musicians came to him to spin their tunes: The Dead, The Airplane, Janis Joplin, Creedence...and they listened to him rhapsodize while waiting for their minute on the air. The simple fact was that Bear needed something fresh to talk about on the air every day, something of our shared reality like car repair, yet something romantic like motorcycles. My motorcycle shop stories made it easy being right now and right here while attracting local celebrities like the Fogerty brothers from Creedence, Country Joe, Sun Ra, Hells Angel Sonny Barger...even UC Grad Student Ted Kaczynski stopped by Mother's Motors in '68 although no one knew then he would become the notorious Unabomber.

Soon realizing that although a genius motorcycle mechanic and a charming guy, my partner in Mother's

Motors and Part's Pile was hell-bent on antagonizing the US government and the IRS. Wanting nothing to do with overt antagonism, I sold my interest in Mother's Motors in '68 to use that money to buy into MC Escher and to throw a few parties like the KMPX SuperBall benefit concert. [see page 125] There were opportunities everywhere, and fabulous people eager to meet, often introduced because of one story or another told over the air. My KMPX benefit largess together with a particular story about my being paid for a BSA motorcycle custom job with a Mother's Motors tombstone brought me together with the people then proposing the Woodstock Festival. One of them had a big thing for BSA motor-

cycles. Their proposed rock festival was to happen in the summer of '69, right around my 25th birthday. I liked the idea which seemed one hell of a way to throw a birthday party.

But that glow of success faded when my girlfriend crashed her motorcycle in front of the Trident Restaurant across the Golden Gate Bridge in Marin. After that, I could not get on my customized Harley Sportster [see page 125] without thinking of Holly's brains splattered over the pavement in Sausalito. She died coked up, her coke dealer friend who had been riding with her, now dead with her. But that dark poetry was not enough. For me, the then-nascent cocaine reality was rapidly becoming an infinite darkness beyond the portal of psychedelia, an abyss, the *OM* in ominous.

On a whim I moved to London to share a friend's neat little house in Nottinghill Gate; so there I was in London, blasting around Mayfair in a chopped Mini Cooper when the mud-fest in Woodstock came down. While in London I concentrated on my interest in the antiquarian book business, buying heavily into Arthur Rackham before returning to San Francisco.

I also bought the Iran rug which figures heavily in this narrative.

Back in California after mid '69 more often than not I opted to run round town in my yellow '63 Porsche 356 Super Coupe. It was an egg yolk that could do 130 mph. A fabulous ride that unfortunately attracted the cops like a magnet! Being mindful as I drove east toward the early morning sun on Geary Boulevard, the smile on a hitchhiker's face simply roped me in. Of course, I'd give her a ride.

"I'm Chantal," she said as she opened the passenger door to become the breath of fresh air I needed! We would spend some good years together.

My 1960s, red Morocco-bound Encyclopedia Britannica presented Afghanistan as an insanely tumultuous place. Pashto and Farsi are the main languages. After a short list of natural resources, a six-page litany of conflict ensues. Lambskins are the big export while nuts, mulberries, grapes, and fragrant Sardas melons are grown primarily for local consumption. Neither opium nor hashish is mentioned in my '68 edition.

I first read those very same pages immediately prior to the seven months I spent in Muslim countries in the early 1970s. I was in search of a particular treasure. That drive-about came to include a month or so in Afghanistan. My companion at the time and I loved our yellow VW Squareback. We could sleep in it comfortably, and it had a very discrete trunk up front. We were on the road, searching.

In 1972 Americans could travel overland from Europe to India in relative tranquility. At that point in time, the Shah still held Iran hostage with American duplicity. It was quiet there although palpably tense. Next door there was a very fragile ceasefire in the on-again-off-again war between India and Pakistan. Their shared border was open only one day a week at Lahore. Timing would be important. The weather would prove a factor.

In August 2001 serendipity brought that jaunt through Afghanistan to mind: First, a museum curator of consequence showed interest in my Afghani weavings; then my Iranian dentist let me in on his family secret. Their remarks prompted me to dig out my photos of the Middle East two weeks before Sally Larsen (my significant other since 1978) and I were scheduled to leave for her September 12, 2001 gallery opening at Chambers Fine Art in New York City. [see page 130-143]

While there in his dental chair, I mentioned our travel plans to my dentist. I included our intention to visit my mother in Washington DC, and inquired on the spur of the moment if he had visited Iran recently to see his own family. While doing a root canal on my tooth, the young Persian captured my imagination when he characterized a family visit to his home south of Tehran.

"The first thing my mother does when we gather for a holiday is to pull out the family pipe and pass it around. After a couple of puffs of opium, we don't feel like killing each other!"

"Opium! Isn't that illegal in Iran?" I asked with a thick tongue once he had removed the mass of gear from my mouth.

"Of course, it is. America coerced the Shah...," the young dentist drifted off for a moment. "It is the biggest mistake. Only opium can keep the Middle East cool. Opinions are too passionate. Too fiery. One mullah issues a fatwā...there's a war."

"Kill Salman Rushdie."

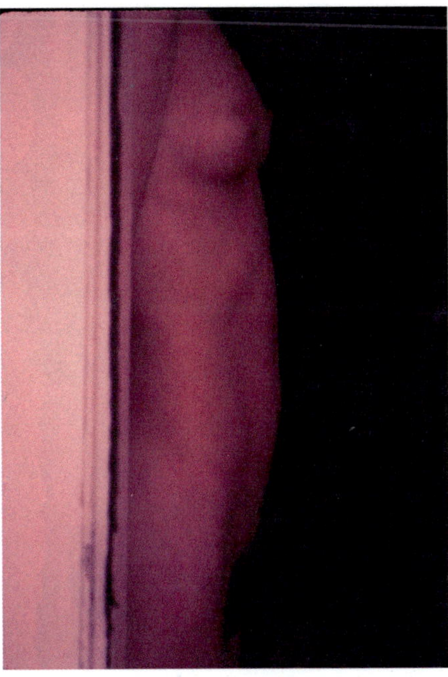

"Exactly! Satanic Verses."

In the weeks that followed, I could not shake the implications of his simple ethnobotanical observation. The dentist's remark offered such a clear lens. It triggered a fresh take on several personal encounters over which I had puzzled for years.

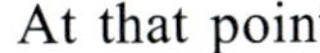

At that point

in 1971/72, I was traveling with an American girl of French extraction. Chantal and I saw ourselves as wanderers seeking ancient threads of culture. To the Muslim merchants along the long road, we were greed-driven infidels seeking treasure, probably Jews with a trick up our sleeves, certainly nothing more than

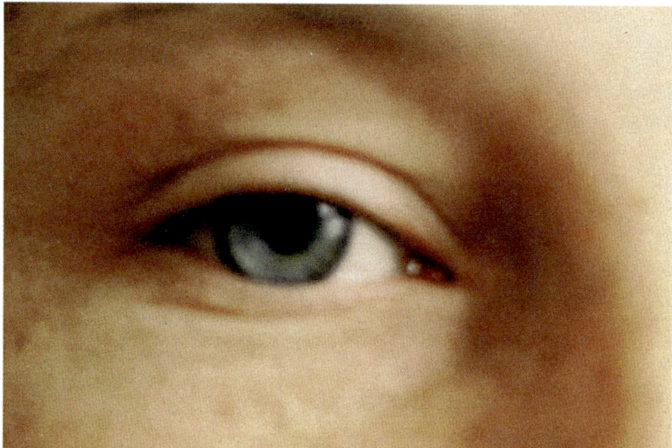

sheep to sheer. By the time we returned to Europe in late 1972, I had decided the oriental carpet business was not for me. The aesthetics of Islam had lost their charm as the attempts to murder, rob, and cheat us accumulated. What had we done to deserve this disrespect? My thoughts were a jumble; my notes were incoherent. I was missing something basic and knew I would only appear naive and biased. So I never bothered to consolidate my thoughts on the Middle East. Besides the whole deal had gone bust. My travel notebooks and my 35mm slides disappeared into a drawer. [see A Reality Check: p 84]

A winning industrial recipe had financed that yearlong, footloose swing through Europe, North Africa, and the Middle East. We had the juice in hand to spend a year traveling before settling in somewhere, maybe New York, maybe Paris. Chantal and I had been on the road in the VW for six months by the time we reached Afghanistan. We spent most of the time in France, Italy, Spain, Morocco, and Turkey although we bounced through Germany and England as well.

We crossed from Iran into Afghanistan in a blinding sandstorm. The Iran-Afghanistan border is notorious for them. In fact, you don't really drive so much as careen over sand swirling in the wake of a fast-moving truck. Our narrow VW barely spanned the sand ridge created by the wider-spaced truck tires. In no time at all, fine sand coated everything inside the car. We could feel it on our teeth. Needless to say, the howling wind and nonstop scraping induced a rare degree of anxiety. Our every prayer was for our air filter.

At twenty and twenty-eight, Chantal and I were Americans on the road. While in search of something cosmic we were currently following a surreal convoy whose drivers knew every turn in the road from the lay of the land. It was a terrifying moment. Nothing prepares you for driving fast while blind. You can only resign yourself to trust.

The truckers were exuberant Afghanis returning home in wildly decorated trucks. Bumper to bumper with several dozen vehicles, we were a moving chain inside the swirling tunnel of sand. The only thing for sure, we were somewhere in space. The road itself was nowhere to be seen. The truckers were sand people accustomed to land as indefinite as clouds. They were nomads with a sense of this place inculcated by a hundred generations. The pace was fast. Shifting sand was not about to interfere with their plans to party in Herat that evening. Indeed, as we had prepared to depart from Mashhad in Iran, the storm was being reported by drivers heading west. The news made the truckers in our convoy heading east ecstatic. We would soon find out why.

Coming through Iran as we were, overland travelers enter Afghanistan on the highway between Mashhad and Herat. There were two roads to Mashhad from Sari on the Caspian Sea; we had taken the northern route which ran close to the shared border with Russia. I had always wanted to see Russia, but never anticipated the view across the border would face an enormous field of Soviet tanks, their big guns aimed at Iran. When I thought about it, unanticipated yes but not surprising, given that Iran was then an American ally!

The jaunt from Sari to Herat is a journey of not so many miles, yet it a bewildering leap in time. At the

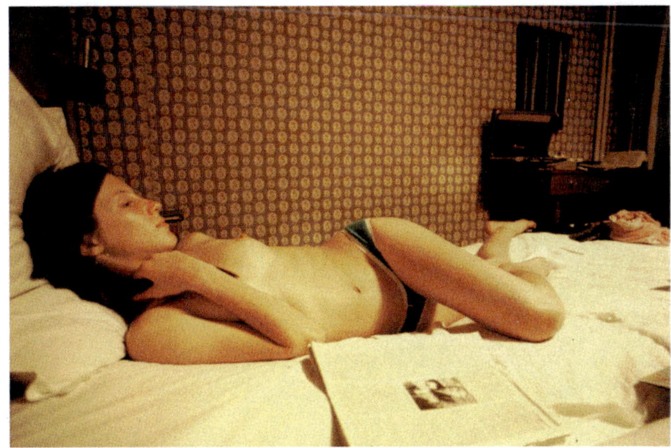

frontier between Iran and Afghanistan, we could barely see the guard shack due to the blowing sand. Inside, dusty border guards in threadbare grey-green uniforms waved us on with a perfunctory stamp on our passports. They were not curious about us, nor were they about to spend time outside searching our car or the trucks. Not in that skin-blasting sandstorm. This is what the truckers in our convoy had foreseen. The keen eye of the fat official sitting on the only chair inside, however, was not to be missed. He would exact his toll on these truckers at a later date. They would pass through his toll gate another time when something would be subject to an unexpected levy. We had been forewarned.

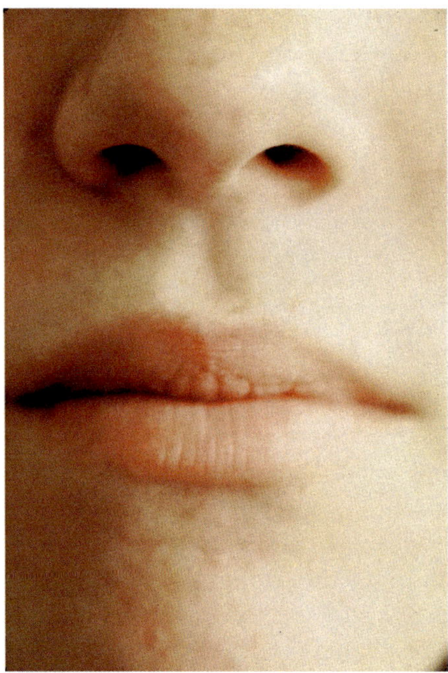

The 200-plus miles between Mashhad and Herat passed slowly, the five-hour drive more exhausting than our occasional 12-hour day. Inside that storm, the unknown was encroaching ominously as if we were nearing the edge of the Earth. After sweaty hours on that highway, the tension broke as the storm subsided. As the sand settled to reveal a perfect cerulean sky, a floral magenta glaze made the desert smile with life in the distance. Low mountains ran to the northeast. Silhouettes of distant camels stood against the southern horizon at times although any people with them were swallowed by the heat shimmering over the sand.

We held our place in the convoy. We had been warned to stop only where trucks were stopped while in Afghanistan. Bandits were said to lurk everywhere which seemed odd as we saw almost no one. We had, however, noticed burned-out cars along the way. There actually weren't that many cars on the bumpy concrete highway, while there were far more trucks than buses. And every one of the trucks was decorated to the max with colorful gingerbread. Suddenly several men in gray pajamas and rag turbans appeared atop the moving truck in front of us. We could not imagine where they had come from at fifty miles an hour, yet not only were they up there smiling at us, they had a huge water pipe with them. Soon we began to notice other people atop the trucks and buses coming at us in the opposite direction.

The two men atop the truck in front of us situated themselves so that they might stare at us comfortably without craning their necks. As if we were curiosities in a zoo, they fired up their hookah and passed it back and forth while pointing to this or that, often Chantal, who seemed to be provoking serious contention. We waved at them, and they at us, as ever smiling. The all-pervasive cloud of diesel exhaust from the trucks kept us from determining whether they were smoking tobacco, hashish or opium. Not that there was space for daydreaming. Without warning, the traffic line would snake sharply into the oncoming lane to pass a donkey cart with automobile tires. The men up top hung on casually.

Nor did the donkeys miss a step as we cleared their carts by scant inches at fifty miles an hour. No one seemed concerned, least of all the cart drivers whose sartorial choice of gray pajamas, long shirt and rag turban were clearly de rigueur locally. While the distant desert shimmered with color, the Afghani men were plain as Quakers. Not having reached Kabul, we had yet to notice the hats of newborn lamb fleece which the Afghanis call karakul.

Once we were several miles clear of the storm, we pulled over with the convoy. The stop was a town on the map although it seemed little more than one petrol station near a small river. Even if surrounded by sand, we were relieved to get out for a stretch. Nearby, the shimmering heat animated the magenta effect we had seen elsewhere. Just beyond the parking area, thinly scattered clumps of low, dusty plants offered up millions of magenta flowers. Up close, the tiny blossoms are nothing special, yet regarded en masse as you see them at a distance, they blaze neon-like across the sand. For me, many things about Afghanistan would prove invisible while close by.

Back on the highway heading southeast, there are no signs, no lights, and few trees. You are on this highway, then you're in Herat. The drifting sand simply becomes dusty brown buildings of plastered bricks or crude Russian concrete. Turkey and Iran had cars and trucks, lots of them; Herat had donkey carts fitted with scavenged automobile tires crowding its streets. We had passed through Kurdish villages in eastern Turkey which were as primitive as Herat, however, they were never featured as major cities on any map.

On our map of Afghanistan, Herat is a big dot; it has a reputation for being ancient. Where western cities

have sidewalks, Herat has open sewers along unpaved streets. One steps over these shallow gutters to enter every doorway, as all have done for several thousand years. The finer establishments bridge these reeking ditches for would-be customers. However, wood being at a premium, these conveniences were rarely more than a flimsy six-inch wide board.

Herat is on the other side of modern. Time and reality are perceived differently there. The Afghani is resigned to the inhospitable nature of the Earth. Where people in the West think to build up into the sky, Afghanis dig down into the earth to escape sand storms and encroaching marauders. Many find water and shelter in this sandstone netherworld as millions have for millennia throughout the Middle East.

The change of pace in Afghanistan allowed the last few weeks before the sandstorm to settle into a different picture of life. That is the way it is when one simply meanders, as we were in the Middle East. Chantal and I were letting one day lead to another. You see what you see as you *keep on truckin*'. We had intended to spend a day or two in Mashhad but the reports of a coming storm had us pack up and go. As a consequence, you are forever catching up with yourself, looping back to reflect on something that passed days before. Something almost missed.

We had been some weeks in the Middle East before getting to Afghanistan. The Bosporus splits the Eurasian landmass at Istanbul. Only eighteen hundred feet wide, the strait is far more than a third of a mile of water. Once on the Asian side of the waterway, an older age suffuses every view and every viewpoint. Six thousand years of local history are still operative. That Islam has been a dominant force for a long time is immediately apparent, yet what that means takes time to sink in. Which, in our case as travelers, translated into miles later. For six months we were forever recalling curious yesterdays while contending with yet another all-new today. Things blur. You miss a lot.

We were longer than planned in Istanbul because of an accident: A truck smashed into our car. Shop time was required to replace the fender and headlight. Braving the crowded streets on foot, we visited the overdone displays of the Topkapi Museum. The literature reports the extravagant building was once a sultan's seraglio. Elsewhere we checked out the Byzantine mosaics in the Hagia Sophia Museum, itself once a mosque and before that a Byzantine church. A church one day, a mosque the next...now a museum. I liked the recycling aesthetic; it seemed efficient. Sadly, the Hagia Sofia was dimly lit and the mosaics were obscured by a wash of mud. A man dressed in rags with his bucket came with us to splash water on them so we might see their designs. It worked...but seemed so weird.

That first night in Herat Afghanistan I was still trying to assimilate Turkey and Iran. Pain, a very specific physical pain, invariably led these musings back to Istanbul.

Mosques abound in Istanbul. Nearby one with an ancient graveyard, while taking a photograph of the monuments, I got the worst bug bite of my life. The sharp bite became a searing pain that lasted for days. Most likely it was a scorpion that left the vicious purple welt on my leg. But there was no stinger in the wound so it may have been a viper. Whatever nailed me, the dark welt would take thirty years to fully disappear.

The physical retaliation for my impropriety should have made me more aware, but it did not. I did not see it as a cosmic warning, just a really nasty bug bite. Nor did I look back at the painful hip-bruising fall I'd taken in Yugoslavia when I nonchalantly stepped onto a slippery boulder at a beach. I had yet to learn to listen to non-verbal clues. More pain would be required.

I was out on the road looking for a clue because I needed to make a few changes. For one thing, I needed to spend far less time in three-star French restaurants

with their fabulous wine lists. I was about to explode. Nothing like a few months on the road in the Third World to starve off fifty pounds. We would be five months getting back to Paris as we made our way to India by way of Switzerland, Austria, Yugoslavia, Greece, Turkey, Syria, Iraq, Iran, Afghanistan, and Pakistan.

Our intention was to drive through Turkey into Syria, then loop north through Iraq to spend a day or so in Baghdad. The plan formulated in Paris was whimsical: Chantal had a friend in New Delhi, so let's go. We could stop in Kabul to see my friend whom we had recently bumped into in Spain, and maybe source a treasure trove of flying carpets along the way. So the trip was not entirely a lark although serendipity was to be our guiding light. I did have contacts in Tabriz and Teheran; I called them and said I was coming. No problem, we'll do great business, yadyada. *Alhamdulillah, Praise be to Allah.*

In a nutshell, the business plan was to source carpets with a very specific design from the renowned weavers of Ardabil near Tabriz in northwestern Iran. Ardabil is ancient, famous for the shrine of Shaikh Safi al-Dinand, and long revered for being so nearby where Noah's Ark was said to have been discovered on Mount Ararat. The small wool and silk rug from Ardabil which I had acquired in London was a 20th-century copy. The huge original carpet woven in 1539/40 and now in the Victoria and Albert Museum is magnificent, but my little copy is as beautiful with its deep lapis blue background. I could have sold it a dozen times, so why not find copies to sell? That was the mission. Seemed simple enough.

The five-hour drive from Istanbul took us to Ankara with its intriguing old city and fascinating museum. The Mahmut Pasa Bedesten, once a covered bazaar, sits just outside the ancient citadel wall on the hill. It is in the Han (Inn) district of old Ankara. The main gallery is 150 feet by 60 feet; ten masonry domes sitting on pillars form its roof. Now the Museum of Anatolian Civilizations, inside the fifteenth-century building, ancient Hittite fertility figurines and intriguing metalwork speak to the origins of modern culture in the Middle East. These diminutive bronze age adepts pioneered the iron age circa 1400 BC. According to our self-described tour guide, the swordsmith Mime who raised Siegfried in Wagner's Ring Cycle learned his metal craft in the Hittite underground warrens. I did not pay too much attention to his details other than to ask myself how long it would take to walk the 2000 miles from central Turkey to Northern France.

South of Ankara, we passed through Polatli and Konya enroute to Mersin on the Turkish Mediterranean. The sea was beautiful, however, we had recently spent several weeks on a beach in Morocco, so we pressed on. At the Syrian border, we had to regroup because the Syrians did not want me to visit their sand pile. They insisted I was Jewish, which I am not, because I have a Jewish name, whatever that is. They insisted my name was on their list as a persona non grata.

It did not make any sense to me that my name should be on any such list. But they said it was and they had all the guns! Unfortunately, what made sense to me did not matter in the slightest at that moment. The border guards were all of sixteen years old with fascist uni-

forms and loaded machine guns. There was no arguing with them. They seemed to have no mind at all, behaving more like dogs trained to bark at anything unlike themselves. Clearly, I was condemned by their presumptions. Nor was this the first time that a very similar scene had played out for us. Once before, when we had tried to enter Libya from Tunisia, I was denied entry because my name was said to be on such a list. Curious, to say the least. Only years later did I find out why.

The forced change turned out all right as otherwise we would have missed places which have given me much to think about subsequently. Kayseri and

Gorome, for instance.

After the four-hour drive from Mersin to Kayseri, the ancient subterranean cities in central Turkey told a lot of story. I had always wondered how people made do before they had cloth for nomadic tents. After turning north from the Syrian border, we visited Gorome and Kayseri which had been carved out of sandstone 4000 years ago. At Kultepe the ancient Hittites had tunneled out the exact inverse of a high-rise by digging straight down into the sandstone of the level plain. These were my first underground cities. They were very extensive and highly interconnected.

Today, tour guides lead you down into them. Steep ladder-ways connect the floors each of which is a labyrinth with myriad rooms. Tunnels interconnect with other distant subterranean developments. Deep underground, their smelter fires torching white hot due to the vertical draw of the tall chimneys, the Hittites led the avant-garde of the bronze age, becoming one of the first cultures to smelt iron successfully. We had been deeply impressed by the Hittite artifacts in the Ankara Museum, and here was their birthplace. Quite obviously, long before either Christianity or Islam, Middle Eastern society was a thriving modernity. The moment made me want to ask the would-be tour guide in Ankara a few questions but that was never about to happen given the miles now between us.

In 1972 when I was there, five stories underground, the ancient sandstone labyrinth housed a disco featuring warm Coca-Cola and the Rolling Stones. Cushions on worn-out truck tires provided seating. The blaring 8-track tape cassette player hooked to a car battery had been "liberated from an infidel" our host proclaimed, which everyone in the room translated instantly to boosted from a car in the parking lot! His innuendo-laden braggadocio induced a wave of anxiety among our fellow travelers. You could smell the tension! Every one of us had left a car full of life support necessities up in the visitors' lot.

If that were not enough, right on schedule, the lights went out. Of course, the battery-powered music didn't miss a beat. Our guide reassured us in an unctuous voice that he had only been teasing, and that surely his associates were merely refilling the gasoline generator which powered the lights. You could smell the crowd tighten up. We had run into this lights-out ruse before in both Morocco and Istanbul. The lights were out for several minutes and the fool kept the jabber going. I never understood this strategy. I could not understand why he felt entitled to do it. I always felt taken hostage. It certainly did not inspire me to leave a better tip.

Nearby in the Valley of Gorome, we came across a painted mural that continues to inspire my speculation. The valley itself is a deep-cut canyon where fast-flowing water had left innumerable giant gumdrops of sandstone, now carved into buildings. Many had flat roofs currently bright orange with drying apricots. Interspersed were orchards of verdant green trees, mostly olives and apricots, but there were also palms.

The church which housed this early Christian depiction had been hollowed out of a natural sandstone formation created by erosion in the gorge. The dimly lit, fourth-century mural inside the church had been painted in earth tones on the sandstone by Byzantine

Christians to commemorate the Biblical creation story. Curiously, Adam and Eve are a hermaphrodite, and the Devilish snake emerging from the Tree of Knowledge of Good 'n' Evil is actually spiraling down a giant amanita muscaria mushroom, the classic red and white, magic mushroom currently regarded as a poison.

As I stared at that wonderful old imagery, wondering how it had survived. I was getting the sense that in these parts, knowledge was considered poison.

We headed north for Ordu on the Black Sea. After dinner overlooking the sea, I woke up in the middle of the night racked with diarrhea and burning with fever. Worried because I was seriously delirious, Chantal loaded our car in the middle of the night and she headed back to Ankara in search of a doctor.

Chantal navigated the dangerous highways back to civilization in the dark while I slumped in the passenger seat. I was peering out through a lens of pulsing blood as the sunrise brought hellish heat. But I could not get space and time to sync. Streaming by mile after mile I could not make sense of the children playing atop the dead water buffaloes floating in the endless canal adjoining the road. The sky, ground, and water were all toned blood red, the macabre rafts bloated round like balloons, the buffalo legs straight up, the happy boys diving off, climbing on, diving off, and on and on and on…

The US embassy in Ankara recommended a doctor who terrified Chantal by asserting that most likely, the poisoning had been intentional!

"Those Black Sea people know good fish from bad," he insisted. "You will be foolish not to consider that you are traveling with more money in your pockets than whole families might accrue over several generations in Turkey. They would happily eat you alive as a slave. Your independence makes you the other, their's to own. In their mind, you are forever the infidel, a slave, property."

"Never appear in public without your dark glasses," the doctor then cautioned Chantal. "They will throw acid in your eyes!"

When I finally came around several days later Chantal confided how this warning continued to terrify her. She could hardly go out she was so freaked. We also knew that if the doctor was right, we had been spared only because she had not eaten dinner because we had been arguing. Truthfully, I don't know why we went on from there. Nor do I know what that doctor gave me to break the fever. I do know that I began losing my hair.

Four or five days later we left Ankara and headed east toward the Turkish-Iranian frontier. A few hours from the Iranian border, the city of Erzurum was crowded when we arrived. A World Cup Soccer Match had the town in an uproar. The dark streets swarmed with men in nondescript robes. They were moving shadows amid blinding dust. Driving was tricky. It did not seem like a good place to look for a hotel.

We pulled into a crowded truck stop for gas and food. I checked the oil and tires, topped off the tank, and parked out of the way so the VW wouldn't get smashed by another careening truck. In the crowded roadside restaurant, astutely presuming us Americans, the owner asked if he might be paid with an American Kennedy half-dollar coin. An effusive man with dark hair, a grand mustache and large dark eyes, he invited himself to sit down with us, bringing complimentary Turkish coffee and local sweets with him. This had happened before on our walk about Muslim turf. Once seated, he swept some crumbs off our table and launched into his opinion.

"I collect Kennedy coins," the restaurateur explained as several wing-clipped quails ran over to gobble the crumbs at our feet. "American Kennedy sent a man to the Moon. This is shared by all men, a proof that Allah is Great."

I liked his style but I did not have a Kennedy half-dollar with me, so I peeled a dollar bill off my pocket roll and let him make change with Turkish money. Our plan had been to eat and run but the gregarious Turk wanted to talk. He kept us there late, a hookah soon appearing, belching tobacco smoke strong enough to kill flies. Then came a salver of *salepi dondurma*, the much-vaunted Turkish orchid ice cream said to have an

aphrodisiac nature. While we had at the deliciously cool, chewy confection with knife and fork, the Turk cut straight to cosmic issues...meaning Allah, of course.

I tried to concentrate on the mochi-like texture of the *salepi dondurma*. It was smooth and sweet and curiously mallowy with an earthy appeal like the deadly

sweet Turkish coffee served with it.

Allah. Allah. Allah. In Algeria, the ultra-devout had been everywhere. In Algiers they were forever beating each other bloody on street corners outside the cafes, always proclaiming Allah, Allah, Allah.

While the greatness of Allah was hard to take too seriously, I had long been a big fan of the space program, so I listened. The rhapsodic Turk never quite demonstrated to me that Allah had anything to do with the success of the American Moon missions, although I did like his vision of the Moon landings as something for all mankind. His was a wider view than my more cynical take on the realities at NASA.

As far as I could tell the Turk's Allah this Allah that was little more than the chip-chip-chip of the quails eating crumbs at our feet. It really did not seem to mean anything. Like our friends in London who say fuck every third word; or Americans genuflecting with Oh My God!

It was dark when Chantal and I walked outside into the dusty evening. Three men in caftans accosted us near our car, demanding dollars and passports. I could smell their adrenaline.

Obviously, they were not going away without something for their trouble. Several months in North Africa and earlier conversations with Chantal's Algerian brother-in-law in Paris had made certain things clear. Something about the Islamic exchange system, which demands that everyone be tested endlessly as a fool, leads Muslims to believe that they can demand tribute. If you are fool enough to pay, then Allah is merely punishing the foolish by means of the faithful.

"Three at a time, they can be dangerous," Ali had

warned.

When the trio spread out, I took stock. I was not feeling all that together after the monster bug bite in Istanbul and the bout of food poisoning in Ordu. I did have a water-filled wine bottle in one hand and a walking stick in the other. I had acquired the camel whacking stick in Morocco, the most pleasant of Islamic places. It was a wicked rose wand with vicious prickles. I bought it in Fez to warn off the parked camels which were forever snapping at us as we walked around. The cane had remained undisturbed in our VW trunk for months until that afternoon when I had rearranged some luggage. Pure whimsy had me take it with me when we walked into that restaurant. Perhaps the cane made them think I was a cripple. In Morocco, they butchered the lame camels for couscous. I had a feeling this trio thought to harvest us, and I knew they would never anticipate how quickly I can adrenalize.

My years among California bikers ingrained patterned reflexes. I wasn't rattled, I just knew I had to connect first. As one man closed in on me from the right, I told Chantal to lock herself in the car and to honk the horn. The men lunged as I spoke, never expecting my thorny stick to tear viciously across his eyes. A second wad of rags came at me from the left where a lucky backhand swing connected my heavy wine bottle with his head. As the first man stumbled away blinded by his own blood, the second dropped like a stone in a spray of glass. In less than a second, it was now one-on-one and I had a weapon in each hand.

The third attacker crept into the shadows.

Having no interest in explaining this incident to

the people inside much less to the Turkish police, we split immediately. Makou in Iran was something like 200 miles of mountain road to the southeast. It was late yet eerily moon bright and fortunately without much traffic. Mount Ararat of Noah's ark fame lay a few miles north of the well-worn highway near the border with Iran. On another day we might have stopped by, but not that night. Clearly, we had worn out our welcome in Kurdish Turkey.

Things were coming in too fast to evaluate: the bite on my leg that was not going away; the near-fatal food poisoning; now an attempted mugging. What's going on? What are we doing here? I knew my violent resolution of the latest incident, and the vehement warning given her by the medical doctor in Ankara, had Chantal totally on edge. Turkey had been hard on both of us. Currently, Chantal was trembling with fear. She had yet to tell me about being grabbed by men while alone on the streets of Ankara while I was recuperating at the hotel. Worried about what might happen if we got stopped, she tossed the blood-stained rose wand over a roadside cliff. I was sorry to see it go but understood her need to do something.

Four hours later we were waved through the border into Iran by sleepy guards who barely looked at our passports. We drove into Maku around midnight.

Under the iron thumb of the Shah in the early 1970s, Iran was holding its breath. The veneer of secular modernization seemed thin as a veil and was likely only held in place by police. Of course, the great mosques were impressive. Yet in spite of their sophisticated designs, they were as repetitious and ornamental as the vaulted churches in Europe with their endless Madonnas. Something larger was missing in Iran, something important about the people. It was too quiet. Or maybe I was missing it, which is what I had to assume, given my total ignorance of their language. Whatever, an angry musk sharpened the air. I felt out of sync, especially after my contact in Tabriz informed me, when I appeared at his office, that contrary to his stated assurances, he could not arrange for me to buy any textiles at Ardabil. He explained that I should have known that any production by such famous weavers would be controlled by their agent in Tehran.

"That is not what you said in your telegrams." I

fumed. I could see it coming, the shrug, the evocation.

"Who could know you would come?" He argued in his own defense, "We're in the hands of Allah."

Allah this Allah that! I was getting the picture that Islam did not entitle everyone to all of the truth. Infidels, of course, being enemies of Allah, deserve nothing. They could never be more than a money bag waiting to be emptied. I was beginning to suspect that I would be making inquiries about Pakistani copies of the Ardabil carpet. I was beginning to think I might not even care. Then you think, OK, The Arabian Nights, Ali Baba, Open Sesame, and you decide to go one step further.

We headed for Tehran, figuring to talk to the flying carpet broker there which, needless to say, turned out to be another dead end. We walked around Tehran, not that there was much to see. I began to notice the social malaise in their eyes as the Iranians considered me and stared at Chantal. They despised her freedom. As the Turkish doctor in Ankara had told her, they hated her for having a passport, and for having her own dollars in her tight Levi pants pockets. But I could see that they hated her for looking at them. She made them feel like nothing...like dirt.

I knew Chantal was getting the picture because she never took off her shades.

A particular moment stands out like it happened yesterday. Somewhere in downtown Tehran, we had been attracted to a modern store by the animated crow outside its windows. Their dress was a mix of modern and traditional. Of course, there were no women to be seen. The elegant neon calligraphy on the store's sign

was alien, but the big neon sneaker told the story. Needing a pair of sneakers, we went inside where I was greeted by a sales girl wearing a tight Grateful Dead T-shirt stretched over huge breasts. As I sat inside trying on shoes, I realized she was the cause of the animated discussions taking place out on the sidewalk. The men were all but coming to blows. When she returned with a pair for me to try on, their eyes followed her every step.

We left Tehran with new shoes and no carpet deals. It had become very clear that I was not going to be able to arrange the weaving contracts I had hoped to arrange in Iran. Maybe, as an acquaintance had supposed, my

best move would be to have copies made in Pakistan. I had an address in Lahore. That would require a drive through Afghanistan and the Kyber Pass into Pakistan. We headed north toward Sari for a caviar dinner on the Caspian Sea only to find that the Shah had sent all the caviar to Europe and America. We had to content ourselves with chicken. And for that, we had to fight off cockroaches the size of your thumb which ran up the table legs and came right onto your plate!

That evening in our featureless room, I kept recalling the Turkish man with a dancing bear whom we had passed by a week or two before in Ankara. Chantal and I had joked about walking around New York with a four-hundred-pound bear on a leash as I sketched the scene in my notebook. What had been so outrageous was that a person tormenting a bear on a big city street in Turkey had been no big deal. That day in Ankara we had been driving in slow traffic. There he was, this man wearing rags and turban, shouting, all the while battering an old bear with a stick while gleeful children danced around tossing pennies. That moment burned into my mind, yet as a drawing, it seemed no more than meaningless circus. I was anxious to see the photograph that I had snapped from the car. Unfortunately, film development would need to wait until we returned to Paris or London.

The next day in Mashhad, bingo, the veil of confusion simply fell away. It was vaporized by a dozen raw eggs served with top open shells and there with the flies on a restaurant table. A courtesy, the eggs had been left there for customers to gulp down raw...or to mix with tepid white rice. A condiment. Undoubtedly, I was hyper-sensitized by the food poisoning incident in

Turkey. Still, that very moment defines a turning point for me, the place, there in the dusty light, sand everywhere, the open eggs, the flies...a realization that no one psyche can embrace it all. That took the pressure off.

The trip to the Middle East was to be a leisurely adventure, nothing too focused simply part of a dream to take a year off to travel to go see a bit of what there is to see. The nuances of Europe, North Africa, and now the Middle East were melding into a drone. There's something fun about sex in strange hotels, still, the day to day was becoming a chore. Beyond that, it was beginning to dawn on me that there is clearly a limit to what you can continue to absorb. Fatigue sets in. Things start going by unnoticed. I don't like that feeling. It can lead to serious mistakes.

Chantal and I had been in London, Paris, Florence, and Barcelona, checking museums, art galleries and fine rug merchants as we traveled. On a whim while in Florence, we had driven south to catch a ferry boat from Sicily to Tunisia. I wanted to go toward Lebanon, but we were denied access to cross into Libya, so we drove west across Algeria into Morocco where we hung out for a month before returning to Europe via Spain. Morocco is the red earth between the Sahara Desert, the Mediterranean Sea, and the Atlantic Ocean. It's fun. Long a crossroads between Africa and Europe, it is a cosmopolitan place with hospitable people, intriguing markets, good food, great hashish, spectacular beaches, and fabulous stories.

On the ferry boat returning us to Spain, I quite literally bumped into an old acquaintance whom I had

known five years before in Aspen, Colorado. An Afghani about my age, Volkmar had been tending bar where I had been hired as a waiter and chef's assistant. This was my first job after my stint as a NASA scientist. The change was OK by me; I was into cooking. Volkmar's connection to the restaurant, on the other hand, was familial: his mother and the owner, both Austrian-German, were old friends. We exchanged notes as the boat made its way from Morocco to Spain.

I was very surprised that Volkmar recognized me. We had not been close friends; I never would have noticed him in a million years. He said my voice had drawn his attention. I was thinking about that when he

blew me away again by asking if I was still a chemist. Why would this guy remember something like that? Then again, bartenders do that. I explained that I was taking a break from science to pursue my interests in European art and Middle Eastern hand-woven carpets. We talked about Spain and went our separate ways when the ferry docked.

One afternoon a month later on the Left Bank in Paris, Volkmar walked into a sidewalk cafe where Chantal and I were sipping coffee. Travelers do have a way of bumping into one another on the road. I didn't think much of it then. He sat down as if we'd planned a meeting. This time we announced our new plan to drive to the Middle East in search of copies of a desirable rug, itself a copy of a famous carpet woven in Iran at Ardabil. Volkmar nodded, thinking carefully before offering to introduce friends in Afghanistan with the right connections in Pakistan. If I could not get what I wanted in Iran, he said that we could always find him in Kabul by asking at the Restaurant Gulzar which he described as a German eatery owned by his mother. I said we would look him up if we made it to Kabul. As we drove north in Iran toward the Caspian Sea, I was glad to have the contact.

Jagged images of the last months on the road, like so many pieces of a jigsaw puzzle shaken together in a box, filled my thoughts as the monotonous miles and long hours rolled by. The heat of the desert between Herat and Kandahar almost finished us. The car needed servicing. The ubiquitous dust was getting to it. We needed water and Chantal needed a restroom. There was nothing as far as the eye could see to the south and only a distant mountain range to the north. Nothing but sand. Few trees, buildings, or even stones of any size. Only sand. You either went with the flow of the trucks, or you became a sand-covered lump along the side of the road. Every once in a while, the wind bypassed a certain spot, allowing a few palms to survive. At these places where everyone stops, amid the carnival of trucks, donkey carts, and camels, you find the same travelers whom you have been seeing along the road since Istanbul.

At one of these stops between Herat and Kandahar, we met two young Americans from the upper Midwest who were walking around the world with a hand cart. This was our first encounter. The smell of peanut butter brought one of them over to our yellow VW where we were eating peanut butter sandwiches made with Afghani bread. A very delicious combo. Peanut butter is regarded with suspicion in the Middle East. We had brought several jars with us.

The brothers were two guys with an idea for a book about two brothers from the Midwest who walked around the world. Although they never stayed anywhere long, they had an impressive scrapbook with all sorts of local newspaper clippings from the year they already had into their adventure by the time we met them. When I said that I did not envy their trudge through the sand storms, they reported the nomads had told them the worst was nearly over. Soon it would be the unrelenting desert heat that would torment them until they reached the city of flies, by which they meant Kandahar. We left them there in the shade of a palm and heard little more of them until we ourselves had driven

to India and back.

By the time we made it to Kandahar, we were fried. Chantal had changed her plugs more than once as we flew down that blistering road at seventy. At one point she leaned back in the seat to be stung by a huge wasp that left a cruel welt. There was nowhere to stop and nothing to do about the pain. It was one of those days.

When we reached Kandahar, it was evening and cooling off rapidly as deserts will. We checked into the Peace Hotel on the main road. After extracting the hideous stinger from Chantal's back, I tried to get some ice from the office. Obviously, our concierge wrapped

in rags did not understand my request because he responded with concise directions to a bakery where hashish cookies might be had, adding that if we wanted hashish to smoke, we should cross the road to the Love Hotel and buy it ourselves because he was too busy. All very matter-of-fact. He said nothing about ice.

As I considered his proposal, he took a big snort of nasty-looking black snuff from an odd little metal box with a bit of mirror on top. Apparently, by busy, he meant it was time for him to admire himself in his tiny pocket mirror because that is precisely what he sat there and did. Back in our room, Chantal said she would live without the ice because her French mystery suave had muted the sting, adding she might die, however, if we did not eat something soon.

Kandahar soon proved to have more than enough flies. They were everywhere amid the stalls in the market. I assumed they spilled out of the open sewers until we turned a corner to encounter an enormous swarm of flies in the middle of the street. They were all over something bigger than our car. Moving, buzzing, black...sinister even. Only after a moment did we realize it was a pile of sheep heads. Butcher shops lined both sides of the street.

Suddenly put off about eating, we decided to go by the Love Hotel to score some hashish. Nothing like a puff of ganja to give the world a rosy glow. We were a little paranoid about trying to score drugs in spite of the pungent swirls of hashish and opium we had encountered along the streets. It was obvious that no one was too uptight about smoking things other than tobacco. Still, we would be discrete.

Turning another corner, we came upon a luminous

display of tiny green grapes neatly arranged on a cart. The delicate white-green orbs passed the waning sunlight like gemstones. They drew us with great promise. Their proud vendor smiled under his rag turban. When we came close enough, he popped a grape into his mouth, beckoning us to follow suit.

The tiny grape exploded in my mouth as pure ambrosia. Never had I ever had anything like it. I offered him Afghani currency; he wagged his finger to indicate another preference. I had a single dollar ready. He snapped it up instantly and gave us more grapes than we could possibly eat. With him beaming after us, we hauled our sweet treasure back to our hotel.

Momentarily satisfied we struck out for the drug lords across the street. On the way, our noses led us to a street stall offering fresh tandoori-baked bread and skewers of charcoal-cooked lamb. We ate standing there, although the flies made us vow to never try that again. Across the highway outside the Love Hotel, a classic 60's VW van painted by hippies leaned precariously with two flat tires. It didn't look like it had gone anywhere for a while. The cryptic psychedelic calligraphy painted across its back door read Dope Trail to Katmandu. The license plates were French.

Inside the Love Hotel, psychedelic posters from San Francisco and New York adorned the lobby walls. They were haphazardly hung as if being anything but level was the whole point. I had once had some of the very same posters on the walls at Mother's Motors, my motorcycle shop in Berkeley, California. Several stoned Europeans draped the ancient sofas like melted licorice sticks. I suspected that they owned the VW bus outside.

A calculating Afghani in an immaculate white pajama outfit watched us from behind his desk.

"You want to fill your fine car with hashish!" The man announced in a booming voice before we ever reached his desk. "Allah tells me these things." The aroma of hash and opium thickened the air. We were clearly in the right place. The stoners on the old sofa didn't move.

"Not exactly," I said, offering a single ten-dollar bill.

Disappointment swept across his face, not that he was going to miss our money. He narrowed his look.

"Of course, one must be careful," he backtracked slightly. "First you see for yourself. Come to heaven. Choose your taste," he threw open the door behind where he stood to reveal a small room filled floor to ceiling with racks of fresh hashish in lumps large and small. Unlike moldy European hashish, this had the fragrance of spicy opium and the consistency of fine taffy. I held up the ten-dollar bill: he handed over a hunk the size of a big oatmeal cookie.

That bit of business out of the way, he drew us closer with a beckoning finger just as the grape seller in the market had done an hour before. The man in white took a Marlboro from a package on the shelf and then snatched off the lid of an oil barrel to reveal forty gallons of dark hash oil the consistency of honey. He was absolutely beaming as if he had opened the door to paradise for us. The fragrance of his pride and joy was overwhelming, indeed. It made our eyes tingle.

Our ecstatic supplier plunged his cigarette into the goo with one hand while adroitly igniting an entire book of matches with the other. He brought the two together in his own face and huffed, hacked and puffed the sagging cig into a cloud of thick smoke. Fragrant hash and opium mingled as he passed the flaming cig to us with the smile of a man in touch with God.

"No better in Katmandu," he assured all the while choking to hold in the smoke.

Of course, we had to give this holy smoke a go! But how to describe that fresh opiated Afghani hash high? Other than WHOOSH! Clearly, this brain candy had more than a mere swirl of opium blended in, a fact apparent by its unmistakable bouquet.

"It is the will of Allah that Afghanistan be the home of the finest hashish," our effusive host proclaimed. "Afghanistan is the mother of the sky. Only here do you find the sky in the stone. Afghanistan is the bluest lapis lazuli, the greenest emeralds, the whitest poppies, and the reddest. We have the golden root tea!"

He went on and on in evermore rhapsodizing tones, proposing the secret of this most perfect of all hashish to be the very same secret of the world-renowned grapes of Kandahar. This little-known perfection he declared to be none other than the sanctified pigeon shit fertilizer gathered inside the minarets of the mosques! A Gift, *Alhamdulillah, Praise be to Allah.* Blessedness to be sold by the mullahs.

The hippies on the sofas didn't move a muscle while we were there. We drifted away with our ten-dollar patty after many a thank you and our promise to stop by upon our return trip from Katmandu.

Outside the Love Hotel, our shadows swam with the passing headlights; not that every car careening along that road had lights. Scary, indeed! Back at the Peace Hotel, our concierge had yet to stir beyond his stool. He was still admiring himself in a mirror the size of a dime when I asked for our key.

Our schedule was constrained by the days on which the border between Pakistan and India was allowing travelers through. We wanted to see the Buddhas of Bamiyan, and I intended to look up my acquaintance in Kabul. Aside from the carpet biz, the idea of a European-style meal, even if German cuisine, was very appealing. We figured to take off right after exploring the open-air markets at Kandahar. The previous evening's delicious grapes had proved one never knew what was to be found.

The cool morning was as ever alive with flies. Great and small, they ruled the air. It was impossible to avoid them. Our only salvation lay in the greater attraction provided by the heaps of rotting sheep heads. Constantly swatting them aside as we perused shops selling colorful powders in glass bottles, we came to a street of ovens and forges with blacksmiths next to bread bakers.

We bought a bag of flat Afghani bread. Far too much to eat ourselves. As ever, the baker wanted a dollar while we only needed a dime's worth. This was an ongoing problem. We simply could not use a dollar's worth of most edibles.

There were far too many flies to eat out on the street. I found myself walking around with a hand covering my mouth and nose. The flies, the open sewers, the rotting heads, the intense light, the teaming streets of Kabul can get old really fast. After looking around for a couple hours we turned back toward our hotel. We cut along a street of tailors where local people were having shirts sewn together from a selection of prefabricated fronts and backs. Chantal liked to sew, so she stopped to buy several of the panels which had complicated patterns woven into the bright white cloth. These exquisitely made parts were said to have been handwoven by the women and girls in the tribal areas outside Herat, Kandahar and Kabul. It was becoming very obvious that little of Afghanistan could be seen from the road.

The tailor, observing Chantal swatting flies, offered me a sheer blue-gray burqa cloak that would have covered her like a tent with a grilled window. "How else to keep away flies?" The merchant proposed seriously in very nicely spoken English. "Very sexy, besides," he shrugged as if merely stating the obvious.

Chantal saw what was being offered and put an end to it, "Oh, no you don't! No bag. I'll eat the flies."

While loading up the car we found out how hot it had been the day before coming into Kandahar. Our stash of candles had melted to soft pools. I knew then the rolls of film stashed with them were fried.

Some hours later and a couple of hundred miles further on, we found an adequate hotel in Kabul without any problems. It also turned out to be in the same area as the only German restaurant. Sometimes you get lucky. We decided to go there straight away. I was eager to explore the potential of Volkmar's weaving connections in Pakistan. Throughout the Middle East, the Pakistanis were known for their willingness to copy anything, or to supply anything for that matter, if one came with the right introduction.

We arrived for dinner at the Restaurant Gulzar before the owner. When she came in, I introduced myself. Of course, I apologized for already having sent back the chicken dish thinking I had been served beef because the meat was so dark and tough.

"Oh, no," she assured me with a grimace. "That is Afghani chicken. Everything in Afghanistan is tough.

"I will let my son know you are here, she added hastily. "Don't run off."

She left us with our supper to go manage her affairs. The restaurant was fairly dark. We ate, puzzling quietly over things that we were too tired to discuss.

Other diners arrived in small groups. Some went straight for reserved tables. Others waited to be seated. Soon the place was quite busy. For the most part, the crowd was a mixed company with the men and women dressed as you might find them in Europe. A good percentage were clearly local, probably diplomats or businessmen; others seemed more likely to be tourists. Snippets of German blended with English, French, and Pashto as conversations swirled about the room. Cigarette smoke thickened the air while faint German music from the kitchen filled in any gaps.

After no more than half an hour, the proud owner reappeared with a beautiful strudel to say we should save room for dessert. She also announced that her son would be around shortly. I don't know why I was surprised she could reach him so quickly.

Perhaps I had underestimated the hashish we had smoked before coming to the restaurant. Something had warped my sense of time, not to mention given rise to insatiable munchies. The hot strudel looked great.

Colorful trails of psychedelic dots followed the proud

owner as she marched her strudel around the room, advising each table to keep it in mind. It was pure circus. Her customers loved it.

When Volkmar appeared shortly thereafter, he paused to pay his respects to another group who had entered only a few minutes before. They peered our

way as he approached our table. Unlike typical Middle Eastern men who do not like to have to consider women, Volkmar said good evening to Chantal by name. His memory and his attention to detail were impressive. Then again, his mother was German. As he sat down, a waiter appeared with a chilled bottle of Rhine wine, a commodity not found easily in Muslim countries.

"I thought wine wasn't allowed," I observed as the waiter poured.

"That is why you find German restaurants throughout the Middle East," Volkmar explained. "We must have our German wine. We have special arrangements, almost like diplomatic immunity."

"We should have looked for one in Tehran. I felt like I needed a drink there."

Volkmar laughed. "We are everywhere, Tehran, Baghdad, Damascus, Cairo, Tangier. Our parents came from Germany after the war. And there were many Germans here in the Middle East before that."

The waiter appeared with plates of warm cherry strudel while Volkmar offered a few suggestions of things to see around Kabul, and inquired about our plans. I almost forgot to speak the strudel smelled so good. I mentioned the Ardabil rug design I wanted to be copied.

He smiled. "Do you have a picture?" Volkmar asked.

"Right now?"

"Yes. He is here tonight. Right now," Volkmar explained. As coincidence would have it, the old man at the other table was the very friend of his who might be able to help find some weavers in Pakistan.

Obviously, these German restaurants were about more than food. While I had better slide transparencies at the hotel, I did have a Polaroid in my shoulder bag. Volkmar passed it along to the other man who immediately joined us for a glass of wine.

The old European was in his seventies, yet lean and agile. His white hair had thinned, of course. His English was fluent, his German eloquent. He recognized the Ardabil carpet and declared immediately that it was beyond the skill of the weavers of his acquaintance. Clearly, he knew fine carpets. While we sipped the wine, he droned on about the carpets he had once owned. It took me a few minutes to realize that he was talking about the good old days between the World Wars in Germany. A peculiar group came to the fore in those years. The old gentleman advised me to reconsider, skewering me with his final admonition, "Leave shop work to cripples." He sat back smiling and let his message sink in.

My idea seemed to irk him. But he did not leave. The old man had pleased himself immensely by stating his conclusion. Maybe he was getting an ornery buzz from the wine. A second bottle appeared. His glass refilled he went on. "There are other opportunities in Afghanistan that might prove more profitable than trafficking in women's work. Wasn't I, for instance, an accomplished chemist?"

Catching me completely off guard, Save Me! Save Me rang in my head like a prayer. This guy is going to offer me a job.

"For instance," he went on as if we were ten conversations into a discussion, "would you be interested in establishing a chemical processing plant nearby Kabul?"

"Processing what?" I asked to be polite, not that I had any interest at all. I meant to become part of the art world.

He sipped his wine while framing his answer carefully. "Natural products… Like your herbal enterprise," he concluded casually.

My heart

fluttered. What was I missing here? Something larger was at hand. His inferences were more than suggestive. This guy knew things. I glanced at Chantal; she was nodding out. Neither of us was used to the wine and hashish, and while I could write off my paranoia as a reaction to the hashish, I was sure that I had not mentioned my failed herbal cosmetic business to Volkmar. In actuality, I hardly knew him. As I weighed my response, I tried to recall our first encounter after five years.

En route to Spain, Volkmar had approached me on the ferry boat from Morocco, saying my voice had allowed him to recognize me. OK, I had been told that by others before about my Midwestern twang. It is like being forever presumed Jewish. Then he used almost the same line again in Paris a few weeks later. The fact was that all I recalled of Volkmar was that he was from Afghanistan. Some other overlap must exist. Someone else.

The facts were that I did know a lot about organic chemistry and that I had tried to start an herbal extraction business in 1968. Sadly, the business had gone bust in San Francisco after I had put a lot of energy into that start-up. What made me nervous was that my life in California postdated my acquaintance with Volkmar! I hadn't spoken with Volkmar since I left Colorado for California. Indeed, I'd had almost no contact with anyone whom I had known in Denver or Aspen since leaving NASA. And guaranteed, during our brief conversations on the ferry boat from Morocco and later in a Paris cafe, we did not discuss business failures. That is not my style.

The old German knew he had thrown me a curve. Clearly, he had done so on purpose. He waited for our eyes to reconnect before checking his gold wristwatch. As his jacket sleeve drew up, his ruby-inlaid swastika cuff links were absolutely impossible to miss. The candlelight set the blood-red stones afire. They were impossible to miss.

"We would seem to have friends in common," I observed.

"It's a small world," he said simply.

Something else was not quite right. Oddly, at that moment I noticed there were no flies around for the first time in days. Somehow, they had killed everyone. I don't know why that made me so nervous, but it did. Like the raw eggs on the table in Iran.

Suspecting it might be unwise to say either yes or no, I waffled. "If the money were right, I might consider a contract. Right now, we are on vacation. A quick trip to see the Taj Mahal after checking out the Buddhas in Bamiyan and the mosque in Mazar-e-Sharif. We'll be back. Of course, you will have to tell me a bit more... before I can say I'm your man."

The old German nodded all but imperceptibly, yet enough to let me know that I had offered an acceptable answer. I watched him walk back to the other table. He certainly carried his years easily.

Volkmar raised his eyebrows cryptically when I looked his way. He exhaled deeply and shook his hand as if something momentous had just transpired. Behind him at the other table, several of the old German's associates cast a quick glance our way. Self-preservation told me to figure out what was going on rather than ask more questions. Indeed, it seemed a good idea to leave before anything else transpired.

We were seriously loaded. Woozy from the wine and hashish, we stumbled back to our room, shadowed by apprehension as we negotiated the dark street with its open sewer. Fortunately, our hotel was not far.

Later that evening the bogeyman of paranoia reappeared. I kept getting flashes of those blood-red stones. I had seen cuff links like that before. Exactly like them! One last puff of the opiated hash and Chantal was gone for the night. The smoke left me seeing things for a while, scanning my mind for any but one other appearance of a ruby swastika. This adornment was no neo-Nazi trinket. Nor was it any ancient Sanskrit

benediction. These were Hakenkreuz, a swastika with blood-red arms running clockwise, the insidious spinning blade of the Third Reich.

None of the one-watt Nazis on a chopped-up Harley Davidson had ever cruised into Mother's Motors sporting these. No, I had not seen these gems on a

biker in Berkeley. It was the old lady in Aspen who had worn them, the old ski resort owner, my employer's childhood friend from the old world. More than once an identical blazing ruby swastika had peeked from under the sleeve of the dark coat which she never took off when as a waiter I had served her dinner at the Golden Horn.

Every mile east seemed to bring me closer to an ominous, all-seeing eye. Nerve-racking, indeed.

To fit everything in we had to hold to a tight schedule. Bamiyan was said to be about eight hours away by gravel road, so the Buddhas and the lakes at Bandimer were an overnight jaunt. Mazar-e-Sharif and Balkh were further away, definitely a two-day loop. Then there was Feyzabad in the northeast with its ancient lapis lazuli mines and equally enduring rivalries. Unfortunately, the day we were leaving Kabul, we heard the Kunduz area was in absolute chaos due to a tribal feud. A bummer. I had a fantasy about walking along a few miles of the ancient Silk Road which passed by Balkh, the birthplace of Rumi, and entered Han China through the Wakhan Corridor. In the 20th century, Afghanistan still shares a border with present-day China; it is a walk that both Rumi and Marco Polo would have made back in the 13th century. It promised to be a romantic setting for a story, but that trek was not to be. Oh well. We had allocated extra days for the lapis lazuli loop so we left Kabul thinking we had time to spare before we needed to head for Pakistan.

Bamiyan was an easy drive, in spite of the fact that it was all uphill into the mountainous Hindu Kush. We did it in a day. The road was dusty and too narrow for trucks to pass in many places. A protocol had evolved:

you join the convoy and everyone moves along at the same speed...no passing allowed. As always, the trucks had people dancing up top, playing music, brewing tea, and smoking water pipes. They moved right along, skidding around turns, spitting stones off the roadside cliffs. We learned quickly that when the truck ahead pulled suddenly to the side to follow suit instantly because another truck was coming through from the other way. I continue to love their music! [see page 80]

The mountains were vast crumbling slopes of coarse gravel and larger stones. Along the snaking road, small valleys and streams would appear. Tall trees and lush grass would revitalize your eye with a welcome swash of green. The city of Bamiyan sat in such a bottom. Sheer sandstone cliffs rose high above the wide valley floor. Low sand buildings, high stone walls, green fields, irrigation ditches, and open sewers filled every square inch.

We followed the map our friend in Kabul had drawn for us to the exclusive yurt motel across the valley from the giant Buddhas. Just driving up to it the view was Awe-inspiring. This is where it all began.

The yurts were the classic circular design, maybe sixteen or eighteen feet in diameter, and domed with fantastically embroidered felt. I had heard about these felt yurt tops. We were ecstatic. Built for international tourists, these modernized yurts had a western-style bathroom which was OK by us. You can get tired of the ubiquitous Muslim squat toilet which is rarely more than a hole in the floor with a bucket of water nearby.

Our host, solicitous because of our well-connected friends in Kabul who had made our reservations, stood by nervously until we said we needed time to freshen up. A bath and a puff of hash seemed just what was required.

"I have new batteries in this flashlight," he said, opening a drawer in a side table while pointing up at the ceiling. "If you want to explore the ten thousand hours of needlework up there to see. this one is very old."

We had found it curious at the time when our friends in Kabul described just where to look for a flashlight. A few more puffs of hash made it all seem just the thing to do.

Tight geometric needlework covered the entire ceiling of the yurt with a million points of color, each

one as indescribable as a distant star. Yet there were obvious patterns and various styles which spoke of hidden stories. Untold hours of careful thought and a wealth of thread adorned the dark felt dome. A family treasure. Equally colorful and complex, woven wool bands decorated every wall, some wide, others as thin as a belt. All women's work. I knew Chantal would burn out the flashlight batteries studying that ceiling. Her kind of thing.

Before drifting away into needlework heaven, a bath and dinner were in order. Chantal was small but she burned a lot of calories. Her brain was forever on fire, tormenting her with questions no one should try to answer alone when only that will do.

It was summer, yet the air was cool high up in the Hindu Kush. From the doorway of the yurt, the serene sandstone Buddha in the distance faced the entire valley which spread out at its feet. It dwarfed everything around. I got out my camera. As I checked the statues with my telephoto lens, the extensive vandalism struck an ominous note. The Buddha's face was totally disfigured, its feet crushed...even so, an aura of tolerant benevolence was sustained.

Outside the sky was lapis blue. Not far from our yurt a bright red opium poppy could be seen in the tall grass. It was an oddity, a late bloomer because the actual poppy season was well along. Not only that, most of the poppies grown in Afghanistan were said to be white. Like angels according to the men selling the black tar in Kabul. In the distance, a call to prayer blared from a loudspeaker.

Our proprietor reappeared to suggest a place for dinner.

"What happened to the Buddhas?" I inquired.

"The will of Allah," our host waved his hand as if that should be enough. I figured that he was not going to attempt to explain. Clearly, from the onset in Mecca and Medina, Islam envisioned leaving its imperial mark where every other religion had flourished, whether Jewish, Christian, Buddhist, or Hindu. In accordance with the Koran, centuries before, the Buddha of Bamiyan's feet and face had been vandalized to show Islamic disdain, much as one dog pisses where another has left its scent. Muslims are forever decrying infidels as dogs, making this pissing contest metaphor strangely apt.

As we stood in the cool thin air, the power of the place evoked a contemplative spirit. I could feel why the contemplative Buddhists had been drawn to the Valley of Bamiyan two thousand years before. I liked being here now. I faded in and out, half listening to our host rationalizing the vandalism of a great Buddha by explaining that devote Muslims felt obligated to destroy idols. The Koran demanded action, he insisted piously. Nearby Kunduz although he could not say precisely where, he had heard tell of a recently constructed concrete highway which had been made of crushed stone Buddhas. Now one could drive across these idols, he jeered. As ever, *Alhamdulillah, Praise be to Allah.*

Our host hastened to add, being in the hospitality business himself, he did not agree with the zealots calling for the obliteration of the great sandstone Buddhas of Bamiyan. Don't get me wrong: Nor did he want them repaired. For him, it was righteous that the faces

had been cut away to prove that Buddhism had no real God able to protect a holy place. To him, these Buddhas were worth preserving to demonstrate that Buddha had no power. "Surely," he concluded, "Allah would strike dead any man who likewise defaced a sacred mosque." His presumption would rephrase itself again and again.

We ate dinner that evening at a restaurant along

the main road through Bamiyan. When Chantal went to ask for a restroom, she returned to say she had been directed out the back door into a hemp field. There were, however indoor facilities for men.

The dinner was as always hot tea, tough bread, tough lamb, and cold rice drizzled with lamb fat. Afterward, we walked along the dirt road where the sweet aroma of hashish and opium scented the cool night air.

Back in the yurt we smoked more of our hash and stretched out on the bed where Chantal took the big 3 D-battery flashlight and swept the bright shaft of light about slowly pausing here stopping there. I just let that be the show while I listened to her thoughts, feeling her searching, jumping, willfully leaping across the cosmos above us, but stopping to carefully absorb a particular woman's story. I could see precisely what was occupying her, it was like I could hear her but not hear her words. It was more that I could sense her logic. Set in motion by extraordinary parents, her keen attention to detail accounted for her precocious ways in the kitchen or when sewing or playing music, or studying anything. As she was now studying what these Afghan women had sewn as their legacy. By then I was aware Chantal needed to see something only once. I listened as the stories in the thread above our bed spoke to her and told me that one day a leap would leave each of us on our own. Chantal and I had met when I stopped my yellow Porsche on Geary Boulevard in San Francisco to give her a ride. She was hitchhiking. That she would simply get out of the car to go her own way one day was always part of that. But I was becoming very attached. As the light of day faded and we drifted toward sleep, I found myself craving her wickedly good chocolate chip cookies.

We slept like a rock in our yurt and got up early to check out the big Buddha. It was billed as the first figurative Buddha. Carved sandstone stairways were so steep they were like ladders that allowed you to work your way up to the level of Buddha's face. I asked our guide why the vandals had not cut the whole statue away if they considered the Buddha such an abomination.

"That it would have been too much work," our guide explained simply. He went on to confirm much of what the yurt hotel operator had said: Muslims were content to have defaced that which the Buddhists venerated. This result, he concluded, was the will of Allah as the weakness of Buddhism was now there for all generations to witness. He did not think it would have been better to leave them intact, and it annoyed him to have me suggest so. This would not be right, he insisted, it would not be an act of devotion to Islam. The Koran demanded idolaters be driven out and that all idols be destroyed.

I didn't think there was much I could say. Then again, we were light-headed in the thin mountain air.

Later that day we drove on up further into the Hindu Kush to see the lakes at Bandimer. We had been warned to stay out of the clear water lakes and streams around Bandimer. Our German friends in Kabul had warned us about parasitic worms like those in certain African lakes. Warm springs from deep in the earth saturate the water with minerals which deposit in many colors along the lakeshore. Over the eons, the deposits have built up into a pool wall that now rises up as if cast out of polychrome concrete. Every place where water spills over the edge, an eternally refreshed rainbow of newly deposited colors glistens in the intense sunlight.

Several French junkies were lounging in a stream nearby, smoking a big bong of opium. Obviously, they

did not believe the stories about the parasites. It was inviting, yet when I looked closely down into the water, I could see all sorts of twitching nymphs and spiraling nematodes. I watched them. The tiny worms sensing my presence, gathered as mosquitoes swarm across a window screen when they can smell your blood. And I suspected that there were leeches around. They were for sale in the local markets.

Beyond the lakes we drove on to see the ancient fortress at Zohak said to be the quintessential existent example of Sassanian brick architecture. Along the way, we passed fields of waist-high hemp, the *cannabis indica* variety used to make hashish, and fields to the

horizon of mature opium poppy pods. There was the occasional late blooming white blossom among them with a red one here and there. No one was hiding anything, that was for sure. There were women out in the fields, talking, watching our car pass. Their silver jewelry flashed in the sun.

At the fortress, a man in dusty cotton pajamas and rag turban gave us the full tour for a dollar. He turned away from my Nikon although he would have talked our ear off for that dollar in English, French, or German. I remember thinking right off that the earth-toned structure at Zohak would make a great country house. It was so romantic there amid emerald fields of hemp and wheat. The penetrating blue of the mountain sky light added a psychedelic sizzle to the colors.

"The Sassanians were Persians, one of the many waves of empire which have swept Afghanistan. *Alhamdulillah, Praise be to Allah*. The final Word of God: We are Moslem, aslama, those resigned to God." Our guide did not seem put off by this as he squeezed the small, yellow-black-striped melon in his hand. He was smiling as he held it to his nose to inhale its fragrance.

Personally, I was not wild about the concept of becoming resigned to anything. These mountains were holy all right. Once Buddhist, then Christian, now Muslim, these mountains were riddled with bullet holes. *Alhamdulillah, Praise be to Allah*!

We smoked some hash in a little pipe while we listened to his stories. His voice was musical, his English European. He would pause occasionally to collect his thoughts. A quick sniff of melon. Always just enough time to let his story sink in while you turned to the panorama. There was little at Zohak to disturb the eye, no signs, nothing painted except our car. Weeks before in central Turkey as we approached on the highway which descended into the inhabited gorges, the drying apricots laid out on the square earthen rooftops had become a vast quilt of orange jewels in the sun. So too had the tiny magenta flowers colored the southern desert to the horizon in the brightness of the Middle East. Now in this thin air and high mountain light, the red poppy here and there sizzled larger than life in a sea of energized green.

"It's so quiet," I observed.

"This is the Hindu Kush," our guide whispered. "This is the quiet between battles."

On that note with a puff for the road, we started back toward Bamiyan in mid-afternoon only to collide with a falling rock minutes later. I saw it coming in slow motion but it all happened far too fast to avoid.

As ever, we were between trucks, and momentarily, on a downhill grade. I watched the stone tumble down the hillside but was unable to miss it when it landed on the road just in front of us. It wasn't even large, about the size of a concrete block. But it was destiny. The truck in front of us sailed right over it. Unfortunately, we caught it with a BOOM THUMP that threw the VW into the air. When we came down a bent beam axle and locked front wheel forced the VW to stop abruptly. That caused an instantaneous chain reaction behind us.

I knew as it was happening that only the skill of the truck drivers could keep us from being killed.

A cacophony of angry horns erupted. The men in the truck immediately behind had seen everything. As

we came to a halt in the dust and gravel, they leaped out of their truck, and without a word, one of them slid under our car. A moment later he shouted to his friend who ran back to their truck for some rope. Peering underneath, I could see that the frame shackle which held our axle beam had been ripped loose. The axle beam itself was more than slightly bent as well. In the US or

Europe, this would demand a tow. In Afghanistan, such conveniences are never required.

The man underneath shouted for those gathered around to lift the damaged wheel off the ground. Once a dozen of us had the corner of the car up in the air, the man underneath cinched the broken parts together with

the rope. He scooted out from under our car, brushing dust off with a smile. The whole event had taken only minutes, even so, I was wringing wet with anxious perspiration. In perfect English, the clever Afghani declared that his patch would get me to Bamiyan. There, he proposed, it could be repaired sufficiently to return to Kabul where it might be repaired completely. I was worried because I knew the frame was bent. I also knew that if I did not get into the car right then, and drive it along no matter how unsafe, these truckers would simply push our VW over the cliff. OK. I offered them twenty dollars. They wouldn't take it. They waved me off as if I had insulted their hospitality and returned to their trucks.

The car drove almost acceptably when going straight, however, it lurched around every turn. Chantal was so nervous I could smell her sweat. Happily, we made it to Bamiyan without incident. When we stopped, the trucker who had helped us before found the mechanic in a flash. This guy appeared with a five-pound hammer and a twenty-dollar smile.

As the truck convoy continued on, the mechanic slid underneath and began banging away. Another man appeared with a heavy wooden box of old bolts and bits of chain. Minutes later, the hammering stopped and the man underneath reappeared, giving me a big thumbs-up. I slid under to take a look. With amazing accuracy, he hammered the frame member back into a position sufficient to stabilize the axle. Then he had cleverly shackled the whole thing together with a few links of chain and a huge bolt.

I was still concerned. Even if this patch got us to Kabul, it was not going to get us to India, much less there and back to Europe. Given the current state of affairs, we were not much inclined to explore Bamiyan further. We left immediately for Kabul where there was an authorized VW repair shop. I had planned to stop there for a tune-up on the way back through anyway.

It was dark when we reached Kabul. We were absolutely exhausted from fretting that our damaged wheel might fall off. Fortunately, the Bamiyan patch had proved quite effective.

We checked into the same hotel room that we had had before and set out for dinner at the German restaurant. Finding my friend there, we told Volkmar what had happened. His mother said their friend owned the VW franchise; she would make a call for us. When she returned to serve our schnitzel, she informed us that we were expected at the VW shop early the next morning.

The VW service manager was a German national who spoke perfect English. After a brief inspection, he announced that both the frame and axle were seriously damaged. We needed to replace the axle, but he could reshape the bent frame members. That is very tricky business on a VW. He was very cordial, as was everyone contacted on my behalf by our German restaurateur. She had clout. Nor was the repair going to be expensive. The service manager volunteered that it was a factory line tow lug that had struck the rock. The lug should have been removed prior to delivery, and that made the mess a warranty repair. The whole thing was going to cost next to nothing, but it would take some time, at least several days. Parts would need to be brought in from Germany. That left us on foot in Kabul.

Surrounded by stark mountains, Kabul is a dusty place with few paved streets or sidewalks. It is divided by the branching Kabul River and several steep hills. Not many of the earthen brick buildings were over two stories. From a distance, the hillsides looked like crumpling wasp hives of crude brick huts with flat roofs made of poles, straw, and mud.

We set out in search of treasure. Most of the rug merchants congregated in the old town near the Kabul River where the bold red patterns of their wares stood out in the bright sun. A surprising number of them spoke very good English. For one thing, we found that we were not going to be able to visit Kunduz area in

the northeast because the warlords were still fighting over turf. The merchants were eager to make the point that we had no option to go into these distant tribal areas to find a better deal. Reporting the bad news from home was clearly de rigueur. The land of lapis lazuli and emeralds is cast by those who live there as a place of perpetual conflict spawned by cosmic forces. It is where the landmass of India continues to collide with that of the Asian continent.

While many of the stalls which specialized in weaving were concentrated in one area, we started to find nice yurt bands elsewhere. We walked every street in the souk bounded by the old city wall, the ancient Bala Hisar fortress, and the river. As we strode along one crowded street, forever amazed by the open bags of freshly ground spices, a hopeful merchant thrust a tiny wooden monkey into my face.

"Japanese," the man announced. "Very old."

The dark carving caught my attention. According to the Chinese I was born in the year of the monkey. I have always been drawn to their antics. I looked at the little guy and knew I should buy him. It was too perfect to dismiss. But who wants something made in Japan when treasure hunting in Afghanistan?

"Ten dollars American," he demanded palm up.

I handed the little monkey back to him and turned away. Ten years later I would come to realize what a gem of a Japanese netsuke that gentle dusty man had offered. It makes sense that the ancient silk routes would have brought many fine things to Afghanistan from Japan as well as from Athens and Venice.

We came across a jeweler in Kabul who had a beautiful chunk of lapis lazuli. I asked if he could shape a round blue marble out of it. He agreed to try, although he was miffed because I did not want any of his stone-encrusted silver jewelry. I just wanted a big lapis marble the size of a big gumdrop. His designs were so clunky I worried that his handmade marble would be anything but round. Yet it turned out nearly perfect, a wonderfully tiny Earth and sky in the round.

Near the jeweler and next to a bread maker, we discovered one of the many gunsmiths working in the souk. With files, hand drills, and a foot-held vise, he fabricated amazing Colt 45 revolvers. He also made percussion cap pistols, modern cartridges being too expensive for Afghanis on camels. It absolutely amazed me that the guy could make a gun with hand tools. I would have bought one of his pistols, but figured it would become a problem at every border. Whenever we passed by I stopped to watch for a minute. One day a boy watching the gunsmith explained that we had just missed the two Americans who were walking around the world. Apparently, they had purchased an old .22 caliber rifle and some ammo. It was the first we had heard of the brothers for some time.

We had some days to wait, so I commissioned a fedora of blond karakul, that being the kinky soft fetal wool preferred by those that could afford the best. Chantal insisted the hat made me look like a pimp. Otherwise, there were plenty of curiosities to keep us occupied. Across the river in one of the newer parts of town, we found some traditional weavers at work.

When Afghani women make their tribal rugs, they produce woven kilims woven without the pile which characterizes carpets. They employ geometric patterns

eerily akin to traditional Native American designs. The city looms didn't weave the yurt bands. That was a country thing. Only the nomadic women weave the long straps used to tie together the traditional circular yurt buildings. A yurt is designed to be taken apart easily, carried by a camel, and then be reassembled quickly. The strong wool straps which hold them together are woven with surprising variety. Both narrow straps and wider bands are used.

Chantal was looking for something to do with her life. She thought she could sell the narrow material in Europe and America as belts. An adept seamstress, she put together a sample with a belt buckle purchased

somewhere in Kabul. It worked beautifully.

As the car repair dragged on, we wandered around Kabul, finding a few bands every day. We ranged quite widely and inquired continually, hoping one of the merchants would have a big pile for sale. It did not seem to be the way things worked. You either got new weavings as they came off a loom, or you got an old one just now being replaced. Some of the oldest pieces had aged beautifully to the muted earth tones of the desert itself. Unfortunately, they were often too frayed for our purposes. Even so, in no time flat, we had more than a hundred yurt straps of the right width. Many of them were fifty to sixty feet long. That meant we had about one mile of two-inch wide wool, something like 1700 belts. At that rate, we were going to fill the VW in no time.

I fantasized about acquiring an embroidered yurt roof. I figured that we could strap it on top of the VW. There was no way, however, that one would be allowed out of the country. As the merchants explained it, that would be like selling a family. Besides, the yurt bands were proving to be enough of a game. To keep track of our growing load we stacked the 2" wide flat coils into a measured pile in our hotel room.

Days went by. The car was not fixed, more parts were needed from Germany. OK, we were having fun looking around, and we still had plenty of hash. The Muslim shrines were meaningless and the Kabul Museum a sad joke, so we spent our days walking the dusty streets. The black tobacco freaks were everywhere, as were the calculating merchants who were forever sniffing the fragrant melons invariably in their hands. It's not hard to figure out why. The open sewers and flies haunted the place, although there are far fewer flies in Kabul than in Kandahar.

We met someone who maintained that he could put together a great pile of yurt bands, enough to bother shipping to the US, for a thousand dollars. I told him that I would have the money wired in and that I would pay him when he showed me the goods.

We were dining nearly every night at the German restaurant. When I explained my intention to have money wired in, our hostess volunteered the name of her banker. I figured we could use the money even if the yurt band deal went nowhere. The very next day I put the bank transfer in motion with a phone call to Europe.

While in London I acquired a letter-size sketchbook and colored pencils. When you are on the road, you are rarely anywhere long enough to have any film developed. I loved my Nikon SLR, but waiting for processing preempted the here-and-now meditation of drawing. This was very much the situation in the Middle East. Then there's the roll of slides that I lost in Algeria when the customs creep opened the Nikon spoiling the exposures inside. Nor were the people of Kabul fond of having their pictures taken by a stranger. Besides, I kept thinking that cameras were a trap for me and that I should concentrate on drawing and writing.

No surprise, when you are stoned and you have time on your hands in a hotel room, colored pencils are just the thing. Prismacolor pencils build up a dense waxy layer of color if one presses hard enough. That colored drawing can then be blacked out with India ink using a cotton swab. When the black ink is dry, the

whole thing can be scratched in patterns with a pin to reveal the colors underneath. Zingo! This is all kinds of fun after a few massive inhalations of A+ Afghani ambrosia. The fragrant smoke, the brilliant colors, time passing freely like when you were a kid playing with crayons on a rainy day.

We spent the heat of the day in our room reading

and smoking. It was nice to sit still for a while. I went for days without taking a photograph. We were going to go on to India to see Chantal's friend, but I was indifferent. My travel focus had been on the rugs from Morocco to Afghanistan. Those prospects were fading. Along the way, we bumped into all sorts of travelers on

the much-vaunted dope trail to Katmandu. It was India versus Nepal: the junkies were headed south for Goa; the hash heads were all spooled up about the mountain spirits of Nepal and Tibet. The fact was that we were tired after nearly seven months on the road. No doubt about it, we were often hiding from one another behind a newspaper or book. There is a limit to what you can take in, even when you are young. And that we were. At almost 21 Chantal was just heading into that high-wire act called your twenties. I was 29 and losing my hair fast.

Chantal found an oddly shaped fragment of a mirror in the bureau of our hotel room. A previous occupant must have left it in the drawer. It might have belonged to a black snuff user who wanted to admire himself in something bigger than the tiny mirror on a snuff box. It was certainly far too large and jagged to carry around in your pocket. Or maybe it was someplace to chop lumps of cocaine into a snortable line. You could certainly buy cocaine easily enough all over the Middle East. I used the fragment of reflection to make a self-portrait.

One morning while walking around the market before it got too hot, we chanced across an extended family of Italians whom we had met previously along the road from Europe. They were traveling overland to India where they intended to load their vehicles onto a ship bound for Australia. A family feast was in the works for that evening in the parking lot where they had parked their caravan. apparently, several more relatives had flown in to join the exodus. We were invited.

The Italians wanted a lamb to roast. They were so charming, we offered to walk them to the nearby street of flies where a butcher would deliver a fresh kill on the spot. There was little refrigeration in Kabul. Minutes later we were in the right district in front of the shop from which our German friends bought the meat for their restaurant. From the live animals held in the back, the old Italian woman with us selected dinner. The ensuing argument between the two butchers over who would get to kill the lamb blew us away. It was too much when you were as smoked up as we were. Knives flashed in the air, shouts, recriminations, each butcher willing to kill the other to determine who got to slit the lamb's throat. In a moment we'd had enough of the marketplace for the day.

That same evening there was a spotlessly clean white Mercedes mini bus with French license plates parked nearby the Italian party. It was curtained like a motor home; currently, a beautiful white Arabian horse was hitched to one door handle. All evening I hoped the owner would make an appearance, but he never showed. There were horses all over Kabul, but I had noticed this Arabian before. Invariably, the Arabian was being ridden by the same lean black rider in flamboyant green velvet. By comparison, the bouncing Afghanis on tired little donkeys looked like tattered midgets. The rider in green made the people on the streets very nervous. You could see them whisper among themselves. Little things draw your attention when you are moving slowly.

Not long after we happened to go to the Restaurant Gulzar somewhat later than usual. That evening we finally encountered the owner's husband. A modern Afghani with his beard neatly trimmed and wearing an

expensive Italian suit, Ferhadi was exceedingly hospitable. We were invited to their table immediately. The Afghanis can smile and greet you with a rare sincerity. Ferhadi insisted that we join them even though they had already eaten. Volkmar was expected.

Taller than most with dark hair and penetrating eyes, Ferhadi began our brief encounter by apologizing that he would have to leave momentarily. A nearly finished glass of tea there on the table before him; an elegant gray karakul wool hat and thin Afghani cloak waited on the chair beside him; I got the feeling that he spoke English, however, he spoke to us through his wife. They spoke German and Pashto, and she trans-

lated. He announced that he had heard about me from his son, and thanked me for being Volkmar's friend when his son was alone in Aspen. He asked if I had enjoyed Turkey and Iran.

"There have been difficulties. I am forever to be presumed Jewish." I shrugged as I watched him study my eyes. A moment passed. He did not launch into a reactionary tirade against Jews. That set him apart. Then again, Volkmar had said that his father was a politician.

"*Wir mögen nicht Amerika,*" Ferhadi turned my eyes back to his. I didn't need a translator to hear We do not like America. I knew enough German to sort that out on my own. Ferhadi watched me carefully as his wife translated to English. "We do not like America." she began. "Muslims hold your freedom of religion to be heresy. Islam will strike Empire America for waging this insult here. When America retaliates with cowardly bombs dropped from planes, as it will, the outrage on the ground will ignite a Holy Fire that will last for a thousand years."

"Are you saying America will get sucked into a holy war with Islam?" I asked incredulously.

"Jihad is not complicated." Ferhadi beckoned the waiter for tea and strudel. "Don't let it stop you from enjoying your dinner. This is not tomorrow.

When you stroll around Kabul see yourself in the Paris of the Middle East." Ferhadi advised.

"Paris? I don't see any booksellers along the Kabul River bank like in Paris," I observed. "Nor do I see anyone debating art and philosophy or science.

"Ah, yes, your Reformation. Your idea of an idea. Being allowed to read the only book which matters:

Islam sorted that out about a thousand years earlier," Faradic smirked. "Most have no need for anything more than the Koran. The Holy Jihad it demands is more than enough for them to think about."

I had to smile. You have to take it with a grain of sand, little more than the bravado of Americans who are forever talking about kicking butt. All over the Middle East and North Africa, Muslims froth on and on about jihad. Every day, throughout the Moslem world in mosques and cafes everywhere, the diaspora reiterates its mantra continuously: The infidel dogs are to be slain, they have no religion; their bitches are to be enslaved, their riches taken booty. The same invectives have been hurled since the Catholic League routed the Ottomans at the naval battle of Lepanto in the sixteenth century. That battle was a turning point, at least it was for Spaniard Miguel Cervantes of Don Quixote fame who was seriously wounded at the battle of Lepanto.

"The seeds are planted," the Afghani elder declared once tea was served and the waiter was gone. "When righteousness blossoms, America will see red."

I projected an oblique reference to opium poppies although I was quite sure he was seeing blood.

"America will see the ghost of Adolf Hitler," Frau Ferhadi added to her husband's declaration. "They will show him on your TV. The lies will create war again."

That did sound about right; America can't seem to get enough of Hitler. To see that, I just had to consider all the hours of World War II footage that I had watched myself. And she was right about another thing: Americans will react to what they are shown on TV.

"You will see this coming, yet you will not know what you have before your eyes," Ferhadi predicted. That's cryptic enough, I thought as he went on. "Our son will see this; Volkmar will understand. This is Islamic destiny."

"Really?" I was intrigued by such an ominous prediction, especially since he had made it so personal. Cafe conversations in the Moslem world often went this way. It is a compliment to be included in the cosmic scale of things. I was curious what Ferhadi would say next if I gave him time. I wanted to know, was he talking about me, or all Americans?

Our food arrived. Chantal and I took a few bites. Ferhadi was reading a note handed to him by an assistant while his wife checked out the action in the kitchen. The schnitzel and potatoes were excellent.

There are thousands of Germans in the Middle East. The fact is German emigration to the Middle East goes way back to the nineteenth century. Many there in the 1960s, however, were once middle-echelon Third Reich executives from Germany who had escaped Nuremberg. They came with their children and brought their antipathy for Jews as baggage. Had this import sown a virulent seed? Was post-World War II, German Nazism the goad that currently had Islam on a rampage to exterminate Jews? Something had destabilized the mutual accord which had allowed Jews and Muslims to co-exist for more than a millennium; something more than the need for a Jewish homeland; something more than Sayyid Qutb's *In the Shade of the Qur'an.*

"Are you saying Islam will build an army to invade America?" I asked skeptically.

"The mullahs say Allah's holy fire will engulf the Great Satan," Ferhadi concluded with a favorite cafe euphemism for America. "There is no room for your freedom to have no religion. The halfway solution is impossible. The devout are to believe as they are told by the Koran."

"I don't see how Islam can attack America. Not significantly," I scoffed.

"There are ways," the elegant Afghani observed wistfully. "See how the Vietnamese peasants thwart American imperial ambitions? They bring down your expensive warplanes with puffs of foil. So too will Islam come as something not easily seen."

"Islam is too factionalized," I argued confidently.

"There are ways to bring people together," Ferhadi

insisted. "Communists aligned with warlords to throw English imperialists and Japanese opportunists out of China."

"OK, so religious war is an inane fact of life," I conceded. Onward Christian Soldiers...kill those godless commies. "What can anyone do about that?"

"It is what America cannot do," Ferhadi persisted. "America cannot allow Islam to be practiced freely because Islam strives to determine government. In Muslim eyes these facts add up to mean that America is a liar. Your Constitution does not allow true freedom of religion because it limits the authority of Islam. The Koran itself declares war on America, as it destines the Islamic domination of your Israel."

"My Israel! That's clear enough."

"When the holy fire engulfs America, your leaders will look for dictators here," Ferhadi went on to predict. "America will not be able to see the righteous coalition building against its ways. America will attack the messengers."

"America was never able to see beyond Hitler," Ferhadi's wife lamented. "America was blind to English meddling in German affairs. Now America supports British colonial ambitions in the Middle East.

I listened and understood what she was saying. I grew up in a German-dominated community in Indiana. I knew basketball was the only thing more popular than racist fascism in the rust belt. "Suppose you are right," I played along even though as far as I knew the English Empire was a thing of the past. "What can the United States do?"

"Americans might open their eyes." Frau Ferhadi's

blue eyes flashed as she spoke out angrily before her husband could answer. Ferhadi did not bristle at her forwardness.

"It is obvious," Ferhadi proposed with a perfectly composure. "America must destroy Mecca and Medina entirely. As they destroyed Hiroshima and Nagasaki. Only this would shake the foundation of Islam."

"Nuke Saudi Arabia!" I could not believe my ears. Up to this point our conversation had been run of the mill cafe repartee from Agadir to Kabul. Surely this was a spoof. Yet there was no smile on Ferhadi's face. He was deadly serious. The readiness of his response as if it were a foregone conclusion put me on guard.

While Frau Ferhadi's interjection had ominous PBS figments of Hitler cascading through my head, I considered how to respond. Ferhadi was waiting for the right question. "What's the solution?" I managed finally.

"Surely, the final solution," Ferhadi concluded with a benevolent smile. "Allah will smite The Great Satan: America will be reduced to dust. Islam will rise in ever greater glory. It is foretold."

"Great strategy for the US!" I chuckled nervously. It was 1972 and anyone with half a brain could see that the USA would never prevail in Vietnam. Another foreign war of consequence would likely break the bank.

"OK. And if nothing happens?" I ventured to keep the ball in play. "Say the Kaaba in Mecca is reduced to smoke and rubble, half of it blown into space, yet America remains unscathed?"

Ferhadi's eyes were fired-up with the logic of his world. "Few here think Allah will prove no more than Krishna, Buddha, or Jesus." He finished with a whisper. "For them, Allah is more than a business. Allah is an obligation, not an option."

I was having a hard time resigning myself to his logic in spite of the fact that the defaced Buddhas of Bamiyan all but made his case. Islam does hold itself to be The Final Solution. How else is one to interpret becoming resigned to God? Or Hitler, or any other wrathful entity, for that matter. "So you propose that America will have to drop the big one to bring about a Muslim reformation? I don't see–"

"Islam is THE Reformation," Ferhadi interrupted. I had to wait for this to be explained by his wife. "And Islam has had its own internal reformations: We have the righteous Sunni and the righteous Shiite as you would have your Greek Orthodox and Roman Church." He noticed my eyes glazing over. I saw him shrug.

"You see why the United States cannot win?" Ferhadi sighed impatiently. Another shrug. "Americans do not take God seriously. You pick a religion as one might select cloth; then have it resewn to fit. Some would go naked, without God. For you, God is optional. Not so for Muslims. Your assumed right to choose keeps you from knowing that Islam is the righteous path. You cannot see that Islam is a serious threat to those who would reject its authority. You do not understand jihad. You cannot.

"Muslims regard your American Constitution as the work of The Great Satan. It is an evil to be expunged. For the devout Muslim, there is no choice, no halfway solution. Allah mandated this war on America more than a thousand years ago. There can be no right to choose God, nor to choose not to submit to God. America will not emerge unscathed: Islam will strike sooner or later. This is the mandate of the Koran. This jihad cannot be avoided. Compromise is not part of the language of the Koran." He checked his watch.

"War is inevitable?" I mused rhetorically as Ferhadi got up to go.

"No! No! If you read OUR history, it began long ago. Americans must resign themselves to Allah. Or they might choose to legalize opium," he added with a wry smile. "Either way, Afghanistan wins."

Time to read the Koran...again, I told myself as his parting comment rang in my ears.

Our car was ready a few days later. Nearly three

weeks had passed in a purple haze. We decided to check out Mazar-e-Sharif in the north. I wanted to see the hemp and poppy fields said to line the roads. Of course, when I went to pick up the VW, it was not quite ready. Another hour would be needed.

There was hot tea and a well-dressed Afghani man in the waiting room. He was a medical doctor trained in Germany with a general medical practice in Kabul. I asked him to describe an interesting case. This, of course, was before the Russians sprinkled the place with land mines. One of his patients had contracted rabies from a dog bite. He had cured the man, with the help of Allah, he hastened to add, by striking the patient

just so on the breast bone. This had caused tiny, brightly colored dogs to flush out of the man's lungs where they perished in the sunlight. *Alhamdulillah, Praise be to Allah.*

The Afghani medicine man was convinced that this had happened. I was flabbergasted. While I tried not to swallow my tongue, I could only hope our car repairs were based on better science.

We had a few details to finish up. Something had our money transfer from Europe hung up. One thousand US dollars in limbo in Kabul. I called the banker in Europe. He said the money had been transferred and sent me a confirmation by telegram.

It was too late to drop off the confirmation at the bank, so we walked over to the jeweler to pick up my blue marble. It proved to be amazingly round for something made entirely by hand. It turned out to be a nearly perfect cerulean ball with only a few tiny stars of gold pyrite. Quite perfect really. Finally, we went to see the cloth merchant with the stash of narrow yurt straps for sale. The tattered bands he had gathered together were disappointing. Not only that, more than half were far too wide for belts. There was the single pile of twenty or so perfect bands set aside, not all new but precisely as ordered. These, however, if bought separately from the rest were each to cost twice as much as guaranteed. I already knew how these merchants thought: the larger the quantity sought, the higher the unit price! Quite the inverse of the wholesale/retail logic that cascades out of The Wealth of Nations.

"Wait a minute. What about wholesale?" I protested.

"If I sell only the best, I will be out of business for

months. I must be treated fairly," the merchant implored with his hand over his heart.

"We'll take the yurt bands that meet our requirements, and we'll pay your usurious price," I protested. "Unfortunately, your Bank of Kabul would seem unable to process my money transfer. You'll get your money when I get it from the bank. If you do business there yourselves, you might tell them to hurry up."

"I might be able to find a few more at this new agreement-"

"No more," I dismissed his offer with a wave. "Every time you will double your price. Tomorrow we will go to Mazar-e-Sharif, then on to India."

"You will find no finer hashish nor better opium amongst those infidels. Here in Afghanistan, you enjoy the hospitality of Allah."

In Mazar-e-Sharif, the hospitality of Allah included a choice of open hemp fields in which to relieve yourself. The only restaurant there also doubled as the hostel. A thick rug was thrown over each table after dinner to make them up as beds. Unlike the kilims we saw along the river in Kabul, however, these thicker rugs were more akin to those of the Caucus weavers. Samarkand and Buchara were not so far away to the north.

The next morning before it got too hot, we checked the car over and drove a bit further. From the roadside to the horizon great fields of *cannabis indica* began just outside Mazar-e-Sharif, continuing all the way to Balkh. You could not smoke the stuff, of course, until it was processed into hashish. Occasionally there would be a field of tall poppy pods waving in the sun.

Here and there a late-blooming red or white poppy blossom was to be seen. The smokable acreage was impressive but really there was little to see but a few ancient mud-and-masonry buildings, the land nearby overgrown with weeds. Of course, a clever guide soon appeared who knew all of Rumi's most quotable lines in English.

Of the twenty or so examples he threw out, he failed to cite the one which occupied me at that moment: "Don't be satisfied with stories, how things have gone with others. Unfold your own myth."

Along the way, as I recall in Paris, Chantal had picked up a paperback on Rumi. She mentioned his insights every now and then. So I was not surprised when she asked our guide, "Can you do Rumi in French?"

And it sounded right.

I picked up her lead and asked him to give us those Rumi lines in Persian; he obliged with a smile and a theatrical bow. I listened carefully to his elegant phrasing, then asked him to do it again, thinking: Yeah, that is what I'm trying to do: Unfold my own myth! And what better place than the Silk Road?

Back in Mazar-e-Sharif, the mosque proved to be as spectacular as it is famous in the Muslim world. Our local guide narrated the tales reflected within each of the geometric constructs. I was familiar with these associations from having studied MC Escher who expressed great affection for Moorish design. Actually, this is the very thing that attracted me to Islamic design in the first place. Our guide, being clever enough to see I wasn't too impressed with that revelation, then let us in on a pious secret, namely, that Allah had turned the local pigeons into angels which accounted for the fact that the birds were all white when those in outlying areas were gray. That story earned him a dollar.

All but invisible in their body bags, the women of Afghanistan disappear entirely when the sun goes down. As that hot summer day cooled, men in fresh caftans appeared beside the reflecting pool of the mosque. Each carried a lively quail in a wicker cage and a hookah. Chatting as they smoked tobacco, hashish, or opium, they encouraged their caged birds to sing by feeding them fat hemp seeds.

As ever, the black snuff users were to be found admiring themselves with their little pocket mirrors.

Local wisdom held that snuff users would die within five years, yet there seemed no shortage of takers. I could empathize. I knew I would resort to extreme measures were I locked into this reality as a birthright.

Fewer people in the north of Afghanistan seemed to be at all interested in talking to us. A quiet person might not concern themselves, but that very thing makes me nervous. Our hotel keeper explained the locals were typically more outgoing. They were, however, preoccupied by a murderous feud currently enveloping Kunduz in the northeast corner of Afghanistan. That part of the world is where the hammer strikes the anvil, our host cautioned us. The suggestion that things could boil over to envelop all of northern Afghanistan in a single day made Chantal and I think it may well be time to leave. Reality felt closing in. That evening in Mazar-e-Sharif our lamb dinner was so tough it proved barely edible, and as ever the cold white rice drizzled with congealed lamb fat was like chewing a candle.

We took off early the next morning. I was craving curry and mango as we headed for the Kyber pass. Much to our relief, the VW repair was proving to be a first-class job No weird vibrations were evident, so that episode began to fade, just one more thing in an ever longer string of this and that. Two hours east of Mazar-e-Sharif a couple of guys seated at the roadside on chairs with guns got up lazily to shake us down. We had been forewarned. Chantal scrunched down in the seat, anticipating a hail of bullets as I blasted on by them at ninety miles an hour. Of course, the trick is to do a little jog that makes them think you are going to

stop so they don't take aim, then while at speed you turn at them unexpectedly, accelerating. That maneuver forces the wannabe bandits to dive out of the way before they can get off a meaningful shot. That had been Chantal's Algerian brother-in-law Ali's advice for dealing with roadside bandits in military uniforms throughout the diaspora. It was proving to be good advice, but

I could never quite get used to the need to set yourself up to run them down. After that, the rest of the drive back to Kabul was just more miles.

Taj Mahal, here we come.

Our dealings with the Bank of Kabul had remained frustrating, although Frau Ferhadi assured me that it

would be resolved. We had enough money in hand, so we decided to straighten our banking out on the way back through Afghanistan. Loaded to the window sills with wool bands and careful to start with a full tank of gasoline, we joined a convoy heading through the Kyber Pass. Once in motion, stopping was not allowed, no stops to take photographs, for instance. Any break-down could spell disaster. Several heavy trucks with mounted machine guns and a dozen armed soldiers in each led our convoy. More brought up the rear. You enter the Kyber Pass thinking you are from America where guns are a big deal. Then you began to notice that atop every ridge, astride a horse, a man in rags is watching with a rifle. Like tarantulas, they watch patiently for days for an opportunity to swoop down on a straggler.

The pass itself was a long winding road through steep barren land. Cannibalized vehicles littered every mile of it. Goats were to be seen here and there; the goatherds were so plainly dressed they seemed moving rocks.

The soldiers were nervous. They knew better than anyone that between the top of the pass and the Pakistani border lurked ten thousand bandits more than willing to kill every person in the convoy for whatever might be gleaned from the carcasses. It had happened more than once. The numerous bullet-riddled vehicles along the roadside testified to the fact.

I barely remember Pakistan or India. Once we cleared the Kyber Pass, we barreled straight across Pakistan because the border crossing was open one day every two weeks. We had no time to spare unless we wanted to stay two weeks. The traffic was absolutely insane. Everywhere you looked, tension was written across the faces. It was almost as obvious as the ubiquitous poverty. Pakistan reminded me of Algeria. I mentioned my observation to the room-service boy in Lahore when he brought an absolutely memorable creme caramel on a silver tray to our hotel room.

"We rent our clothes," he volunteered in perfect English by way of explanation, bowing as he left.

We left early the next morning. At the border, the uniformed Indian women border guard pushed her hand down inside my pants without one word of warning. I never carried our money, but not finding anything, she never bothered to check Chantal for a money belt.

We knew she wouldn't.

We headed for Delhi where we meant to contact Chantal's friend. It was hot and humid. We sped across the vast Punjab floodplain on the elevated road. Brown pampas grass spread to the horizon in every direction. Where there were trees, there were endless green parrots and innumerable people in pajamas carrying water. Halfway to Delhi, we rented a hotel room with air conditioning, only to find the electricity had failed. So no air conditioning, not even a fan, but more than enough mosquitoes. We could not sleep so we took off long before dawn. We wanted to get a jump on the traffic.

Being able to go fast enough to enjoy the wind proved treacherous. Everything overlaps on the byways of ancient India. Fortunately, our headlights caught the fractured glass on the road ahead of us in time for me to navigate the glass and bottles strewn across the narrow highway. A truck had rolled over. The driver sat atop the rig, watching, smoking, waiting for who knows

what. No attempt had been made to warn incoming traffic.

In India, one sits by and watches karma play out.

It was almost dawn by the time we cleared that sticky wicket and got up to speed. Not long after we were slowing down again, this time being directed by policemen to swerve around a pedestrian now squashed flat as a shadow in the middle of the road. We passed this hapless soul slowly, the body was not covered, a surreal sight, indeed. Obviously, the man had been hit hours before in the dark and had been run over many times, enough to flatten him out like a squirrel on a busy freeway. Who needs a camera? Some things burn into the mind forever.

In Delhi, we took a nice room in a grand old English Imperial period hotel. The place had a very nice restaurant and several shops in the lobby. I found a big book on Pahari miniature painting and a Penguin Classic paperback Koran at the bookshop there. Chantal found several Agatha Christie novels and arranged with the concierge to send a note to her friend by courier. We lugged our books back to our room still savoring the tandoori chicken and curry. Several hours later I exploded with major colitis. It was not the same as the problem in Turkey, but it was very disabling.

In the morning, I went to a doctor who worked out of an office in the hotel. He proscribed a tincture of opium that plugged me up when I took enough. Chantal liked the tincture herself; she found it just right for reading mysteries. We lay around, holed up while my system calmed down. Chantal read about Miss Marple; I floated through opium dreams where wisp-like threads of cosmic colors tied together vignettes of incomprehensible schemes. The first few days we hardly made it outside, and when we did finally give it a go, the street scene was equally incomprehensible. I was weak. I knew Chantal was going nuts, but I could hardly move. Days passed, and we got out more and more, but it took ten days to normalize. I don't remember much but one dream.

Each drift into the dream sequence began as opium swept me away. It started peacefully, smoke-like purple and green swirling into a gem-like sphere, turning luminescent photo blue, a round blue ball spinning, spinning, here and there star-like spots of LED red, the glowing sphere swirling, purposefully blue. Prior to New Delhi, at this point, my opium dreams would fade into sleep. Not so in New Delhi where a new chapter locked onto the repeat cycle: Suddenly, the blue sphere spinning, I am inside a metal box. The ambiance is blood red. Wheel wells suggest I am in the back of a huge step van. Paranoia intrudes. Struggling for air, I reach for the rear door handle. I open the door and step out into a disturbing blur of pulsing orange-red and yellow. An infinity of cars is stopped in line at a gas station somewhere, probably in California. I'm in the middle. My eyes search for someone familiar. I cannot discern their faces. They are waiting anxiously in the blazing sun. The drivers are watching television in their cars. My ears pound with the beating of my own heart. I cannot make out what is going on. Now the cars are exploding. Buildings explode. Ships explode. Bigger buildings explode. People explode and explode and explode.

That got old fast. The recurring nightmare made it easier to ease off the laudanum. When my opiated haze subsided, it was very clear to me that I was not going to get much more out of traveling until I had had some time to sit still and assimilate for a while. Our reality was, unfortunately, that we were halfway around the world, far away from anything like home.

Chantal's friend in Delhi had been married for several years. In response to her note, his parents came to see Chantal at our hotel. She was expecting her friend, of course. We never did see the guy. The man's mother said that it would be very inappropriate for them to meet ever again because Chantal had once promised to marry the guy only to later renege. No consideration for the fact she was all of twelve at the time. Apparently, the guy, 22 at the time had taken it all quite seriously.

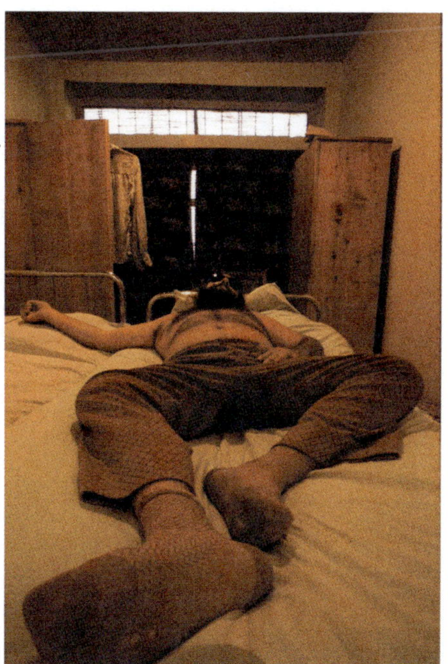

We meandered around Delhi for several days but I don't recall much.

We ran into a couple of travelers with whom we had had fun months before in

Morocco. They planned to winter in Katmandu. I was not much interested in going further. We had talked about selling the car in India, but the war between Pakistan and India had everything up in the air. The Indian border guards had noted the VW in my passport, which meant I would have to account for it when exiting the

country. An official sale could require weeks of paperwork, so we were going to have to drive the VW back to Europe, or give it away and lose the money waiting for us in Afghanistan.

There was also the feeling that I needed to go back to Kabul to straighten something out. Besides the money problem, I needed to know precisely how the old Nazi in Kabul knew anything about me at all. Rubberized by the opiates, I lay on the hotel bed in Delhi reading the Koran, thinking about religion, east versus west, Islam versus everyone, taking notes while Chantal was going over the edge.

We were tired. After a while, you simply cannot take any more in… We turned back having never made it to the Taj Mahal.

We stayed at a different hotel when we got back to Kabul. The Aryana was an old English colonial hotel with the most amazing tiled bathrooms. Among the required amenities, our spacious hotel suite featured a huge Victorian tub on clawed feet and a charming wood-fired water heater.

When you ordered a bath, the chatty concierge would arrive with a basket of fragrant cedar which soon had the tiles aglow with luxuriant warmth. The pleasant conditions were important. We had been warned to stay off the streets, especially in the afternoon. Ramadan was in full swing, so the local zealots were all spooled up. The hotel lounge was full of tourists and businessmen. The latter was there to do business with the government. One of them, an English nurse, provided me with a large bottle of Doctor Brown's tincture of opium that kept my colitis in check.

Unfortunately, the Bank of Kabul was looking

more and more like it was never going to pay out our thousand dollars which even they now admitted had been wired in. I had thought this would have resolved itself while we were in India. Obviously, I was going to be forced to call in the Germans if I wanted our money. On the positive side, the banking glitch seemed a perfect rationale to excuse myself from doing business of any kind in Afghanistan. We went to the German restaurant on our first evening back in Kabul.

Frequent diners are creatures of habit. The septuagenarian with ruby cufflinks was there as expected. He nodded when he saw us. We sat at our usual table in the corner, ordered the usual schnitzel, and described our banking dilemma to the owner. Frau Ferhadi volunteered to go to the bank with us the next business day, meaning whenever the bank decided to open during Ramadan. She explained that this might take a few days given that it was Ramadan with a royal celebration also at hand. She cautioned me to be patient.

I mentioned my interest in attending a *buzkashi* match. She turned away shaking her head in dismay. *Buzkashi* is polo played with a dead animal instead of a ball and mallet. Basically, it was a melee wherein a hundred tribal heroes on horseback vie to be the one to drag the bloody beheaded lamb carcass across the goal.

The moment Chantal took off for the lady's room, the old Nazi was at our table. Anticipating this, I had told Chantal to take her time. And what do you know, the old man spoke perfect English as he sat down.

"We want you to help us process opium and hashish into pure, medicinal substances. And we hear that you have a synthesis to make cocaine of the finest

pharmaceutical grade. We will compensate you well."

"I would hope so! These are narcotics."

"They have legitimate uses," he scoffed. "Only wine, pigs, carrion, and blood are proscribed. The Koran advocates the value of every one of Allah's creations. Other arbitrary proscriptions are expressly banned."

"Really?" I was skeptical. If it were true that the Koran proscribes the banning of anything save for what Allah himself had proscribed by name, that fact would have the DEA sweeping water uphill with a broom forever. Though interesting, the suave old Nazi's proposition brought a more pressing question to mind. "Who

suggested I might be receptive?"

The old man said nothing.

"OK. How about initials?" I was joking but–

"L.L." he said without any hesitation.

"Hmm...I know several," I puzzled aloud.

"Colorado," he added cryptically.

"L.L. in Colorado...doesn't ring a bell," I insisted, asking myself if this guy could know Larry Lasker. "What I might know how to synthesize is of no consequence. Driving people crazy is not my thing. No one who knows me well would ever think I would manufacture cocaine. Coke has made a fool of too many friends. I'm a hippie. My herbal recipes create tonics, lotions, maybe the occasional magic potion."

"We think Afghanistan can become a leading center for production and refinement. We appreciate your unique experiences. We offer a straight business deal."

"I'll keep it in mind. I'm not so sure what Chantal will say...I kind of like it here. There is something very romantic about this worn-out place," I added whimsically. My easy tone let him relax. "Aside from that, there seems to be a problem getting the Bank of Kabul to hand over a lousy thousand dollars which I had wired in from Europe to buy wool yurt bands. I don't get it the bank acknowledges the receipt of the transfer."

"Banking problems can be handled," he said. "Muslims have their own way." Rising as Chantal returned, he acknowledged her politely and went back to his own table.

The waiter delivered our food. Across the restaurant, another stranger glanced our way again. He was seated with two women both of whom I had seen in our hotel. I had noticed his eyes. Little would escape him, and he was clearly watching us. The thought occurred that he might be some kind of cop. Interpol maybe. Given the nature of the old Nazi's proposition, his scrutiny made me apprehensive. That evening, I first noticed him watching us when Chantal left for the rest-room. At first, it seemed he had merely tracked the old Nazi across the room to pass time. When Chantal returned, I realized he was clearly more interested in her. I didn't say anything; I wasn't much interested in hearing about my supposed proclivity for jealous fantasies.

Two days later the same man engaged Chantal in our hotel lobby. Apparently, from what she told me he had learned from someone else about her interest in local weaving. Straight away, he offered his services as someone with just the right connections. Chantal came back to the room with the report. She liked to flirt, but she was not dumb. She knew it was very odd that he had been asking around about her. I didn't like it at all. Something sounded all wrong, but our concern did not last long. By the following morning, Mister Weird had vanished.

Rumors were circulating when we walked down to the lobby. We were getting going late that morning, so we did not see anything. The English nurse who had given me the Dr. Browns reported that she had observed men carrying out something heavy wrapped in blankets. The speculation was that the girls with Mr. Weird the night before had overdosed.

I found that very hard to believe. I had spoken with those girls. You run into people over and over along a long haul like the trek from Istanbul to India. Everyone goes through the same border stops, gas stations, road-

side cafes, and hotels. Serendipity brings you together. These girls had railed against drugs when I had asked them jokingly whether they were on the dope trail to Katmandu or Goa.

The fact was that those two girls were evangelicals, Bible thumpers with big tits. They had convinced themselves that men willing to stare at their tits could be brought to Jesus. I wasn't convinced. I asked the daytime concierge if the police had been called in. The toothless old man smiled. He assured me that the hotel owner had taken care of everything...whatever that meant.

On Monday we stopped by the American Embassy

to see if they would put any pressure on the bank on our behalf. The attaché said there was little he could do. Out of curiosity, I asked if he had heard about the missing girls. He shook his head as he painted a grim picture. "The embassy has a long list of American women missing in Afghanistan. We cannot assume that all have found husbands. Women need to be very careful here. Afghanistan is a very dangerous place to flirt."

Afghanistan is a hard place. Clearly, while the old Nazi might have been able to handle the Bank of Kabul, I was not doing so well. Either the banker was never there, or my inside connection was nowhere to be found. I knew Frau Ferhadi was willing to help because she had already walked over to the bank with me several times. Of course, when we arrived the banker had stepped out moments before even though he had promised to stay.

My own strategy put on another kind of pressure. I went to every cloth merchant with yurt bands that we wanted. I gave each ten dollars to hold the lot with the balance to be settled when our money was handed over by the bank. I also gave each merchant the banker's name and suggested that they call on him at the Bank. Otherwise, our last few days there were spent watching faces. The people did not like having their photographs taken so I just tried to take in what was to be seen.

The burqa-veiled women often stared at Chantal. You could see them turn to watch her in spite of the fact that you could not see their eyes. Chantal was small and free. Her blue eyes and dark hair were not unlike their own, yet she had none of the lines of fear that etched their faces. Years later the world would come to be haunted by one of those girls, Steve McCurry's blue-eyed girl in a red cowl.

We walked through the local markets in the mornings. With a short ride on one of the local buses, our circuit included several nearby villages, one famous for its blue pottery. After a while, we had lined up something like 250 bands, maybe 4,000 saleable belt lengths.

As we walked around, some of the girls said hello to Chantal. A phrase or two might even be exchanged. The only girl who ever said hello to me, however, was struck immediately in the head by the older woman with her.

A few nights later and finally asleep after yet another annoying day at the Bank of Kabul, we were blasted out of bed by an enormous disturbance. War seemed at hand! Outside our window on the quadrangle in front of an official building across the way, several army tanks raced wildly around and around. Men in rich robes cheered as the careening machines tore up the pavement, knocked down trees, and mashed nearby cars. Our Kabul friends had warned us that the King's parties often got out of hand.

It had not taken long for me to figure out to whom the old Nazi had been alluding. L.L. The long shadow sent a chill...and a strong signal. A fresh resolve to redefine myself as an artist and writer settled in as we played out our last few days in Kabul. If the old man had given me the initials PW in Aspen, I would have put it together in two seconds. L.L. took a while. Wolf was dead, killed when his small plane crashed en route to Aspen to see his biker friend L. L. I had known them both, Wolf far better than Lenny. And I knew their friend Hunter Thompson. These guys loved guns. They

loved to drink and drive and shoot. Who knows what tall tales Wolf might have spun once they got the nose candy going? Wolf might have known the old Nazi, but that would not have surprised me at all. I had met his father, but the connection may not have been familial.

Wolf got around on his own. I found that out when we shared a house in London in 1969. Dangerous shadows, indeed.

The old Nazi never mentioned my stint with NASA; those would have been the stories that Volkmar might have relayed. No, there was a larger web out

there, a bigger eye watching. One thing was for sure: if I was not willing to turn my scientific skills to biological warfare for the US Government, I certainly was not going to join the Islamic Reich of Kabul as a drug chemist. Danger lurked an exit strategy would be required: a dangling yes. If put together cleverly, I suspected that we would liberate our funds immediately and gain time to get out of the country with the wool bands. Fortunately, I was in the mood for schnitzel.

The ruby cufflinks arrived minutes after we had assumed our usual table. Appearing the instant Chantal made for the toilet, he did not sit down this time, rather he concerned himself with a hand-lettered announcement posted on the wall nearby. Finished, he acknowledged me with a nod.

"I will call Wolf's friend as soon as I can get back to Paris," I explained, discretely confirming his confidence. "Unfortunately, the Bank of Kabul is holding us up."

"Travel safely," he said simply and vanished.

The next day we had our money. When we came into the bank early, as we did every day, the director came forward to greet our intermediary, the German restaurateur, with an astounding revelation.

"Forgive me, Frau Ferhadi. How could I know this would inconvenience our mayor?"

Our friend was livid, her anger palpable. She knew that he had seen her there with us before, and that he had cared nothing for any inconvenience to her. Pressure had to come through her husband. She was annoyed, as she must often have been living in Muslim society. I was relieved. At that instant, I knew we were going to clear customs with our collectibles.

That morning we heard that one of the American brothers walking around the world had been killed by bandits in the Kyber Pass. The merchants holding yurt bands for us could not wait to tell us the story about the brothers who had stumbled across a hold-up in progress. Apparently, some Kyber bandits were holding a busload of people at gunpoint while robbing them. The brother with the gun had thought to run off the bad guys with a shot in the air. Obviously, these boys had watched too many movies. Not to be driven off their prize, several of the infuriated bandits charged with knives drawn. They overwhelmed the brothers in a wave. While they forced the unarmed one to watch, the bandits hacked his gun-wielding brother into pieces.

We had had about enough of Afghanistan. Any merchant who tried to raise his prices one last time was immediately told to keep their precious bands. Several chased after us, pleading as we walked away, but I had lost all patience. We cleared out of Kabul by noon and rolled into Kandahar that evening.

Chantal and I made it back to Paris in record time. Each time as we approached a border, I put a twenty-dollar bill in the back of the wagon on top of our stash of wool. It worked every time.

Driving straight through Iran and Turkey, we returned by way of Corfu in Greece where we enjoyed an afternoon swimming. We took the auto ferry from Igomenitsa to Brindisi on the coast of Italy. Our cash was running low so we were moving fast. Starved for certain things, however, we resolved to swing by Vivali, our favorite gelato place in Firenze, and to see a movie on our first night in Paris. We caught Clockwork Orange on the Champs-Élysées, Halloween night, 1972. Then we spent a month in London before returning to San Francisco.

Chantal went her own way about a year later. I was devastated. I found it very hard to let go of someone I simply loved and greatly admired for the way she could tell stories and just do things with her hands, whether playing music, cooking or sewing. But I knew I was seeming old to her; I was feeling old myself. It was time to turn a corner.

By the Yom Kippur war and the Arab oil embargo

of 1973, I was well on my way to being bald. To keep from forever having a sunburn, I took to wearing hats. I tried all sorts but settled on the crocheted beanies I had collected in Morocco. Colorful, easy to wash, and hard for the San Francisco wind to blow off, these simple hats became a personal fixture like my beard. I'd look at myself in the mirror and recall a remark by a Berber on a beach south of Agadir in Morocco: "You don't have to be religious to see the wisdom of covering your head from the sun."

I took to wearing a red beanie to art functions, my homage to Monet's spot of red. Yellow became my preferred color for daily wear, while I've black beanies with a single red stripe for business meetings.

"Around 1975 I swapped the yellow VW wagon for a watercolor portrait of it parked in front of the Caffe Trieste. I was spending a lot of time in North Beach with the literary types then known to haunt San Francisco. Eventually, that yellow VW caught fire and burned to a crisp on Polk Street.

Writing fiction and speculating in art came to occupy my time although I have continued to explore aspects of theoretical science. New people filled my phone book. Yet, it was an old friend who was to become the love of my life. We took up surfing which became what eating once had been. This changed the shape of things, especially me.

As if life were a circus of serendipity, a friendship made in the Trieste Caffe had finally provided a rational explanation for my name being on persona-non-grata lists in the Middle East. It wasn't my name at all; just the same name.

A billionaire theater owner from San Francisco put

it together for me when he asked if I was related to the Wehrenberg family which owned Wehrenberg Theaters in Saint Louis where I had been born. Apparently, those Wehrenbergs were active in the Middle East. He said I resembled the owner so much that he had presumed that I was this Wehrenberg's son and therefore Jewish. I wouldn't know, I never met the man. Nor would Marshall Naify be the only Hollywood person to ask if I were this popular Midwestern impresario's son. Director Roger Corman famous for his Edgar Allan Poe films with Vincent Price was another. Nor would these guys be the last to presume me Jewish.

Becoming resigned to God did not lead me to Islam. Even if the chattelizing mullahs of the Arabic languages were to reestablish opiated Islam, Moslem self-regard as the final solution would fail to appeal. I guess that is why Islam continues to rely on proselytizing with a sword. Nor did becoming resigned to God incline me to reconsider Christianity. Clearly, were I to seek the solace of architecture, I would seek out a temple. For me, the resignation seeded by this trek through North Africa and the Middle East boiled down to the fact that I was to be in each of their minds what others would presume me to be. This was immutable in spite of their presumptions having been established by what they had come to assume before they could shake my hand. The truth be damned.

Things are not as they seem. Cycles of stars and planets are required for clarity to emerge. Meaning often comes later, like what was to be learned from the vicious bite I received when intruding indelicately through the boneyard in Istanbul. Risk is always at hand, and death is equally close. By Kabul, I was getting more aware, or so I thought. I did not know how close we had come to the edge until years later.

During the winter of 1979/80, we were staying in the rainforest on the north shore of Kauai. Sally Larsen and I were just starting our life together as a couple although we had known one another for almost ten years already. Graham and Susan Nash had let us use their wonderful surf shack retreat where I came across a paperback entitled Serpentine. It had been left by a previous visitor. Around then, the Islamic revolution in Iran had taken American Embassy staff hostage, and there was a Soviet invasion

of Afghanistan. It was the beginning of an avalanche. Following the Russian withdrawal from Afghanistan in 1989, the Berlin wall would come down. The godless commie empire would disintegrate into Muslim versus reactionary Christian states. Clearly, Islam was on a roll. Sally and I had no idea then how much this would come to shape our lives. We were having fun.

I dug into Thomas Thompson's true crime thriller while torrential rain beat down on the corrugated metal roof of our shack. Serpentine is a murderous tale set in Asia, India, and the Middle East which tracks the escapades of Charles Sobhraj, a con man and serial murderer who savaged unwitting travelers. There is a photograph of Sobhraj in the book. Immediately familiar, his face quickly fell into place as the man watching Chantal and me in the Restaurant Gulzar in Kabul, the man who had stalked Chantal to offer his services as a guide. As the US Embassy attaché in Kabul had said, Afghanistan is a very dangerous place to flirt...

*****

It's live and learn...A Travel Note:

I started out with two great cameras, a Nikon FTN and a Nikonos, plus fifty rolls of 35mm color slide film. Expecting to return with 1800 pictures, I made it back to Paris with less than 200 photographs. Most were lost to postage failures from Italy, Morocco, and Turkey. Others were ruined by customs agents opening my cameras and the film canisters. I did not know how to prevent this until it was all but too late. Clearly, I should never have let my cameras nor my film out of sight.

Retrospectively, I should have had a better plan. I needed some sort of press credential, but also I should have taken much better notes, each carefully recording the time and place of every shot I took.

September 11, 2001

A beautiful day in San Francisco, as it was in New York City. We got a pre-dawn call just after the first plane hit the World Trade Center. A local early riser who thought we were due to fly out that morning for Sally's opening in New York City rang us to say turn on your TV! Shortly after that, I was on the phone with an associate in Manhattan as he watched the second plane hit the WTC from his apartment window in TriBeca. Sally and I saw the World Trade Center die on TV; then we went surfing because we could not take any more bad news. No doubt about it, Sally Larsen's New York gallery exhibition scheduled to open September 12, 2001, was destined to be stillborn.

By the time we got home from Ocean Beach, we heard that general aviation was suspended. We would not be able to reschedule a flight for a week. When we did get to New York City smoke and dust still filled the air. It reeked of burning organic matter as it blanketed the Chelsea district several miles north of ground zero. You could feel it on your skin. The abrasive nature of the grime sanded the black outer surface off my shiny new clogs. I couldn't believe it. We visited our friend Terry Winters on White Street closer to ground zero. Having heard the plane fly directly overhead, he had felt death's closeness. A pall shrouded the city, but a show of great strength in the impromptu memorials. As devastated as Sally was about her exhibition, she knew her loss was only a setback. Others had lost everything.

Once again bitter old men had imposed the death penalty, as ever in the name of God. War and rumors of war have ensued, also in the name of God. It is enough to make you question whether any moral authority can contribute anything save for greater crimes.

A couple of years later while walking back from the Post Office, I was feeling trapped. Reality had sunk in. Our own aspirations lay in ruins with the Twin Towers. I had just read Tarek Heggy's essay about the lack of (and the need for) words for compromise or for integrity in Arabic languages. At that moment I came across her face once again. The compelling blue-eyed Afghani girl in the red cowl was there on the sidewalk, a pretty face on a trampled bit of paper. The photograph made Steve McCurry famous. I picked her up, as ever profoundly touched by her beauty and desperation.

An apprehension that never abates shapes my sense of the Afghani girl's plight. More than ever, it would seem that vehement American reaction in the Middle East will play into an orchestrated dream. Clearly, theocratic Islam requires jihad to survive. Jimmy Carter and Ronald Reagan were too savvy to take the bait. Maybe because they do not take religion seriously, the Bush League smacked the tar baby; they never saw the strings attached to big oil in the Middle East.

HAPPENINGS: Then to Now

1962 August: a car wreck in Ohio changes my life...
1965/67 NASA and Aspen...and on to San Francisco.
1968 I conjure a key trade secret which pays and pays.
1968 I buy MC Escher & discover Moorish design.
1969 Woodstock festival; US astronaut on the Moon.
1973 Arab Oil Embargo...Islam looms.
1973 GUI, Graphical User Interface for computers.
1974 Nixon signs 55 mph National Speed Limit Law.
1975 I produce Deep Relaxation recorded therapy LP.
1979 Khomeni leads Islamic Revolution in Iran.
1979 American Embassy staff taken hostage in Tehran.
1979 Soviet Union invades Afghanistan.
1984 Will Ball games for Apple II; MacIntosh debutes.
1984 My UAL *United Magazine* **inro** article reaches millions suggesting the potential of fine art writing.
1885 The Well online community opens a floodgate.
1987 Intifada begins in Palestine.
1989 Defeated, the Soviets retreat from Afghanistan.
1989 Berlin Wall collapses, US claims Cold War win.
1990s USSR fractures into competing factions.
1990s Solo Zone Publishing founded to establish a trademark in the emerging online kiosk era.
1991 Shock and Awe! But Saddam Hussein hangs on.

1993 I describe ebooks in ***An Interactive Novelist's Wishlist*** in *New Media Magazine*.
1994 Yahoo founded by David Filo and Jerry Yang.
1994 Amazon founded by Jeff & MacKenzie Bezos.
1994 I put Jeff Bezos in touch with Filo & Yang.
1994 The Well expels me for my SZP online kiosk!
1996 Taliban embraces Osama bin Laden's Al Qaeda.
1998 Al Qaeda bombs US Embassies in Africa.
2000 Al Qaeda bombs USS Cole in Yemen.
2001 **9/11** Al Qaeda destroys NY World Trade Center.
2002 US invades Afghanistan, hunting bin Laden.
2002 Tarek Heggy *Our Need for "A Culture of Compromise*": www.mideastweb.org/compromise.htm .
2003 US invades Iraq, justifying itself with Words of Mass Deception, these WMDs engendering antipathy.
2004 Al Qaeda bombs commuter trains in Madrid.
2004 US announces a trillion dollar lithium resource in Afghanistan which had been kept secret by Russians.
2005 Al Qaeda suicide bombers target London.
2006 Twitter founded in San Francisco.
2008 Obama elected by a Shepard Fairie HOPE poster.
2009 Obama fails to close Guantanamo.
2010 American ends military mission in Iraq. WikiLeaks reveals the true cost of the war in lives.
2016 Trump elected. American prestige declines.
2020 COVID! Trump ousted!
2021 Exhausted...USA withdraws from Afghanistan.
2021 Amazon KDP gets everything right, finally !@#$.
2022 I find Ahmad Bābā's fatwā from 1619 online.
2022 PROC and Taliban sign lithium mining deal.

The Trek
mentioning cities on our map

~ 114 stops in the order visited
some for a night, some for weeks
occasionally * car camping

(1 Dec 71) San Francisco, California.... London, England.... Paris, France.... Geneve, Switzerland.... Frankfort, Germany (VW).... Dusseldorf.... Nancy, France.... Dijon.... Perpignon.... Barcelona, Spain (boat).... Palma de Mallorca.... Barcelona.... Avignon, France.... Geneve, Switzerland.... Paris, France.... Bordeaux.... Foix.... Barcelona, Spain.... Valencia.... Arles, France.... Digne.... Geneve,

Switzerland.... Zurich.... Milano, Italy.... Firenze.... Solerno.... Cocenza.... Catania.... Palermo.... Tunis, Tunisa.... Constantine, Algeria.... Oran.... Fez, Morocco.... Erfoud.... Marrekech.... Essoura.... Agadir.... Goulimime.... Agadir.... Marrekech.... Agadir.... Mirleft *.... Marrekech.... Agadir (beach)*.... Essoura Tower

*.... Marrekech *.... cedar forest near Fez*.... Ceuta.... Cordova, Spain *.... Madrid.... St Sebastian.... Casteljaloux, France.... Paris.... Amsterdam, Netherlands.... London, England

(15,000 miles, 1 June 72).... Paris, France.... Dusseldorf, Germany.... Paris, France.... Andermatt, Switzerland.... Innsbruck, Austria.... Spital.... Zagreb, Yugoslavia.... Dubrovnik.... Lake Titograd.... Skopje.... Grevená, Greece.... Igomenitsa.... Corfu.... Vólos.... Thessaloniki.... Kassandra penisula.... Kavála.... Istanbul, Turkey.... Ankara.... Silifke.... Mersin.... Goreme.... Ordu (food poisoning!).... Samsun.... Ankara... Sivas... Erzurum.... Makou, Iran.... Tabriz.... Teheran.... Sari [Shani].... Mashad.... Herat, Afghanistan.... Kandahar.... Kabul.... Bamiyan-Bandier.... Kabul (VW frame repair!).... Mazarisharif (2 Sept 72).... Kabul.... Rawalpindi, Pakistan.... Lahore.... Ludhiana, India.... New Delhi.... Lahore, Pakistan.... Rawalpindi.... Kabul, Afghanistan.... Kandahar.... Herat.... Mashad, Iran.... Teheran.... Makou.... Sivas, Turkey.... Istanbul.... Thesseloniki, Greece.... Igomenitsa.... Pescara, Italy *.... Florence.... Geneve, Switzwerland.... Paris, France (Halloween).... London, England.... San Francisco, California (34,000 miles; Dec 1972)

is an original POCKET BOOK edition.

Moroccan Red Poppy

Middle Eastern \ Indian music CDs

> ***VIRTUOSO FROM AFGHANISTAN***
> SFW CD 40439
> Usted Mohamad Omar

> ***A Meeting by the River*** WAL-CS-29-CD
> Ry Cooder & VM Bhatt

> ***Tabla Tarang***: Melody on Drums CD SF 40436
> Kamalesh Maltra & Trilok Gurtu

> ***Debashis Bhattacharya*** IAM*CD 1007
> with Samir Chatterjee

> ***Raga Pahadi Jhinhoti***: IAM*CD 1081
> Debashis Bhattacharya & Swapan Chaudhuri,

> ***The Drummers of the Nile*** CD-PIR1147
> mahmoud fahl

> ***The Greatest Hits*** CDNF 150478
> usted zakir hussain

> ***krishna lila*** six degrees 657036 1066-2
> dj Cheb i Sabbah

> ***Saradamani*** WLA-ES-23 CD
> Vishwa Mohan Bhatt

> ***Hookah Café*** Triloka 2506-2
> music of Marrakech, Istanbul & Cairo

Afghan White Poppy

The Koran "a sketch for my mother" * page 101

1: The Exordium

1:1 In the name of Allah, the compassionate, the Merciful, Praise be to Allah, Lord of Creation, the Compassionate, the Merciful, King of Judgement Day! You alone we worship, and to You alone we pray for help. Guide us to the straight path, The path of those You have favored, Not of those which have incurred your wrath, Nor of those who have gone astray.

2: The Cow

2:1 As for unbelievers, whether you forewarn them or not. they will not have faith. Allah has set a seal upon their hearts and ears;

2:98 'whoever is an enemy of Allah, His angels, or His apostles, or of Gabriel or Michael, shall make Allah Himself his enemy: Allah is the enemy of the unbelievers.

2:112+ Who is more wicked than the men who seek to destroy the mosques of Allah and forbid His name to be mentioned in them...?

2:115 To Allah belongs the east and the west. Whichever way you turn there is the face of Allah.

2:178+ It is decreed that when death approaches, those of you that leave property shall bequeath it equitably to parents and kindred.

2:207 But there are those who would give away their lives in order to find favor with Allah. Allah is compassionate to His servants.

2:213 Mankind was once one nation. Then Allah sent forth prophets....

2:223 Women shall with justice have rights similar to those exercised against them, although men have status above women. Allah is mighty and wise.

2:229 Divorce may be pronounced twice, and then a woman must be retained in honor or allowed to go with kindness.

2:282 Believers, when you contract a debt for a fixed period, put it in writing.

3: The Imrans (Mary's father)

3:24 For they declare: 'We shall endure the fire of Hell for a few days only.' In their religion they are deceived by their own lies.

What will they do when We gather them altogether upon a day which is sure to come, when every soul will be given what it has earned with no injustice?

Say:.. 'Lord, Sovereign of all sovereignity, You bestow sovereignity on whom You will and take it away from whom You please. You exalt whomever you will and abase whomever you please. In Your hand lies all that is good;

3:142 No one dies unless Allah permits. The term of every life is fixed.

4: Women

4:7 Men shall have a share in what their parents and kinsmen leave; and women shall have a share in what their parents and kinsmen leave; whether it be little or much, they are legally entitled to their share

4:10 A male shall inherit twice as much as a female.

4:34 Men have authority over women because Allah has made one superior to the others, and because they spend their wealth to maintain them. Good women are obedient. They guard their unseen parts because Allah has guarded them. As for those from whom you fear disobedience, admonish them and send them to beds apart and beat them. Then if they obey you, take no further action against them. Allah is high, supreme.

4:73 Let those who would exchange the life of this world for the hereafter, fight for the cause of Allah; whether they die or conquer, We shall richly reward them.

4:73 The true believers fight for the cause of Allah, but the infidels fight for idols.

4:96 He that leaves his dwelling to fight for Allah and His apostle and is overtaken by death, shall be rewarded by Allah. Allah is forgiving and merciful.

4:117 The pagans pray to females;

4:159 Because of their iniquity, We forbade the Jews good things which were formerly allowed them; because time after time they have debarred others from the path of Allah; because they practice usury—although they were forbidden it— and cheat others of their possessions.

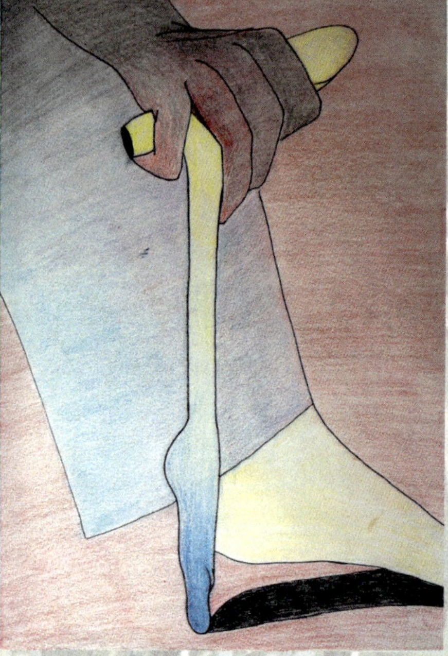

5: The Table

5:03 You are forbidden carrion, blood, and the flesh of swine; also any flesh dedicated to any other than Allah. You are forbidden the flesh of strangled animals and of those beaten or gored to death; of those killed by a fall or mangled by beasts of prey....

5:04 They ask you what is lawful to them. Say: "All good things are lawful to you."

5:33 Those that make war against Allah and his apostle and spread disorders in the land shall be put to death or crucified or have their hands and feet cut off on alternate sides....

5:37 As for the man or woman who is guilty of theft, cut off their hands to punish them for their crimes. That is the punishment enjoined by Allah.

6: Cattle

6:32 The life of this world is but a sport and a pastime.

6:37 All the beasts that roam the earth and all the birds that wing their flight are communities like your own.

6:37 Say: 'When Allah's scourge smites you and the Hour of Doom suddenly overtakes you, will you call on any but Allah to help you? Answer me if you are men of truth! No, on Him alone you will call; and if He please, He will relieve your affliction. Then you will forget your idols.'

6:70 Avoid those that treat their faith as a sport and a pastime and are seduced by life in this world.

6:104 Do not revile the idols which they invoke besides Allah, lest in their ignorance they should spitefully revile Allah. We have planned the actions of all men.

6:138 They [unbelievers] say: 'These animals and these crops are forbidden. None may eat of them save those whom we permit." So they assert. And there are beasts which they prohibit men from riding, and others over which they do not pronounce the name of Allah, thus committing a sin against Him. Allah will punish them for their invented lies.

6:145 Say: 'I find nothing in what has been revealed to me that forbids men to eat of any food except carrion, running blood, and the flesh of swine.

9:14 Make war on them: Allah will chastise them through you and humble them. He will grant you victory over them and heal the spirit of the faithful.

9:71 The true believers, both men and women, are friends to each other. They enjoin what is just and forbid what is evil; they attend to their prayers and pay the alms-tax and obey Allah and His apostle.

15: Al Hijr

15:1 They say: 'You to whom the warning was revealed, you are surely possessed. Bring down the angels, if what you say be true.'

16: The Bee

16:63+ Allah sends down water from the sky with which he quickens the dead earth. Surely in this there is a sign for prudent men.

21: The Prophets

21:6+ We have destroyed many a sinful nation and re-

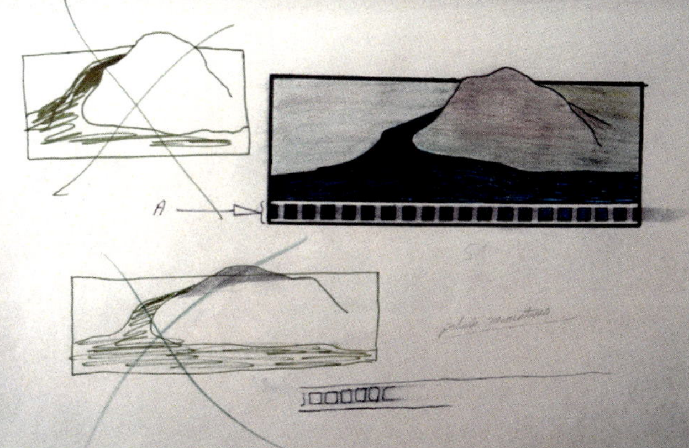

placed them by other men.

24: Light

24:1 The adulterer may marry only an adulteress or an idolater; and the adulteress may marry only and adulterer or an idolater.

24:6 If a man accuses his wife but has no witnesses except himself, he shall swear four times by Allah if he is lying. But if his wife swears four times by Allah that his charge is false and calls down His curse upon herself if it

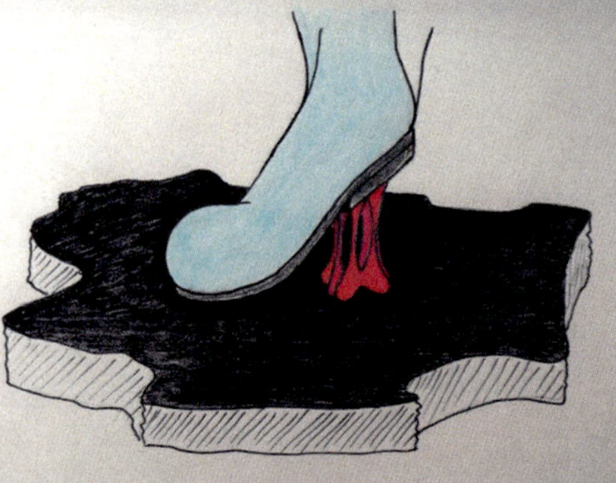

be true, she shall receive no punishment.

29: The Spider

29:1+ He that fights for Allah's cause fights for himself. Allah does not need his creatures' help.

29:41 The false gods which the idolaters serve besides Allah may be compared to the spider's cobweb. Surely the spider's is the frailest of all dwellings, if they but knew it.

31: Luqman

31:1 These are the revelations of the Wise Book, a guide and a blessing to the righteous, who attend to their prayers, pay the alms-tax, and firmly believe in the life to come. These are rightly guided by their Lord and will surely prosper.

33: The Confederate Tribes

33:40 Mohammed is the father of no man among you. He is the apostle of Allah and the seal of the Prophets. Allah has knowledge of all things.

33:49+ Prophet, We have made lawful to you the wives to whom you have granted dowries and the slave-girls whom Allah has given you as booty; the daughters of your paternal and maternal uncles and of your paternal and maternal aunts who fled with you and whom you wished to take in marriage. This privilege is yours alone, being granted to no other. [Mohammed had 9 wives plus slave-girls]

35: The Creator

35:33 They shall enter the gardens of Eden, where they shall be decked with pearls and bracelets of gold, and arrayed in silk....where we shall know no toil, no weariness.

39: The Hordes

39:1 Had it been His will to take a son, He would have chosen whom He pleased out of His own creation. But Allah forbid! He is Allah, the One, the Almighty.

39:25 We have given mankind in the Koran all manner of arguments, so that they may take heed. We have revealed it in the Arabic tongue, a Koran free of faults, that they may guard themselves against evil.

41: Revelations Well Expounded

41:1 This is revealed by the Compassionate, the Merciful: a Book of revelations well expounded, an Arabic Koran for men of understanding.

41:38+ Those who deny Our word when it is preached to them shall be sternly punished. This is a mighty scripture. Falsehood can not reach it from before or behind. It is a revelation from a wise and glorious god.

42: Counsel

42:35 Those who avenge themselves when wronged incur no quilt. But great is the guilt of those who oppress their fellowmen and conduct themselves with wickedness and injustice. These shall be sternly punished.

47: Mohammed

47:3 When you meet the unbelievers in the battlefield strike off their heads and, when you have laid them low, bind your captives firmly. Then grant them their freedom or take ransom from them, until War shall lay down her

armor.

47:3 As for those who are slain in the cause of Allah, He will not allow their works to perish. He will vouchsafe them guidance and ennoble their state; He will admit them to the Paradise He has made known to them.

48: Victory

48: Say to the desert Arabs who stayed behind: 'You shall be called upon to fight a mighty nation, unless they embrace Islam. If you prove obedient you shall receive a good reward from Allah. But if you run Away, as you have done before this, He will inflict on you a stern chastisement.'

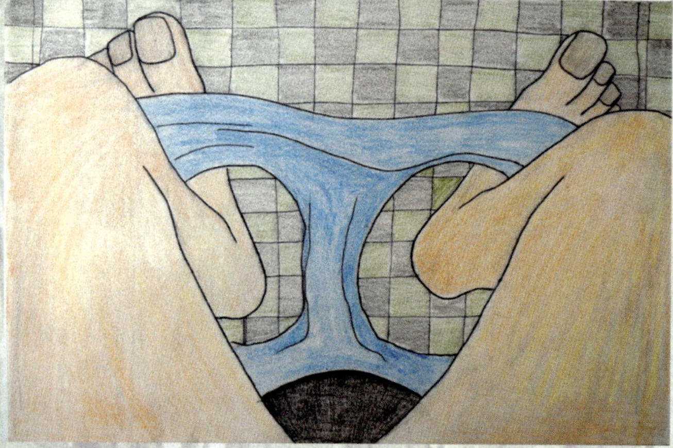

49: The Chambers

49:18 He is watching over all your actions.

51: The Winds

51:53 I created mankind and the jinn in order that they might worship Me. I demand no livelihood of them, nor do I ask that they should feed me.

52: The Mountain

52:1 By the Mountain [Sinai], and by the Scripture penned on unrolled parchment; by the Visited House [Ka'ba], the Lofty Vault [sky], and the swelling sea, your Lord's punishment shall surely come to pass! No power shall ward it off.

52:20+ Fruits We shall give them, and meats such as they desire. They will pass from hand to hand a cup inspiring no idle talk, no sinful urge; and there shall wait on them young boys of their own as fair as virgin pearls.

54: The Moon

54:12 We have made the Koran easy to remember: but will any take heed?

55: The Merciful

55:1 Which... repeat sequence: He created man from potter's clay and the jinn from smokeless fire. Which of your Lord's blessings would you deny?

55:41 The wrongdoers shall be known by their looks;

55:41 But for those that fear the majesty of their Lord there are two gardens...planted with shady trees.... Each is watered by a flowing spring.... Each bears every kind of fruit in pairs.... They shall dwell with bashful virgins whom neither man nor jinnee will have touched before.

58: She Who Pleaded

58:1 Those that divorce their wife by saying so and afterwards retract their words shall free a slave before they touch them again.

60: She Who Is Tested

60:1 Believers, do not make friends with those who are enemies of Mine and yours. Would you show them kindness when they have denied the truth that has been revealed to you and driven the Apostle and yourselves out of the city because you believe in Allah, your Lord?

64: Cheating

64:13 Believers, you have an enemy in your wives and children: beware of them.

66: Prohibition

66:9 Prophet, make war on the unbelievers and hypocrites and deal sternly with them. Hell shall be their home, evil their fate. [Jihad!]

68: The Pen

68:5 Give no heed to the disbelievers: they desire you to overlook their doings that they may overlook yours.

70: The Ladders

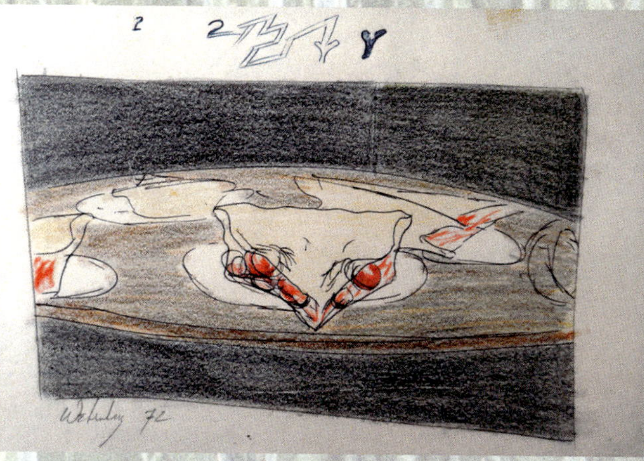

70:22 ...who restrain their carnal desire (save with their wives and slave-girls; for these are lawful to them); he that lusts after other than these is a transgressor...

72: The Jinn

72:16 If they pursue the right path We shall vouchsafe them abundant rain, and thereby put them to the proof.

76: Man

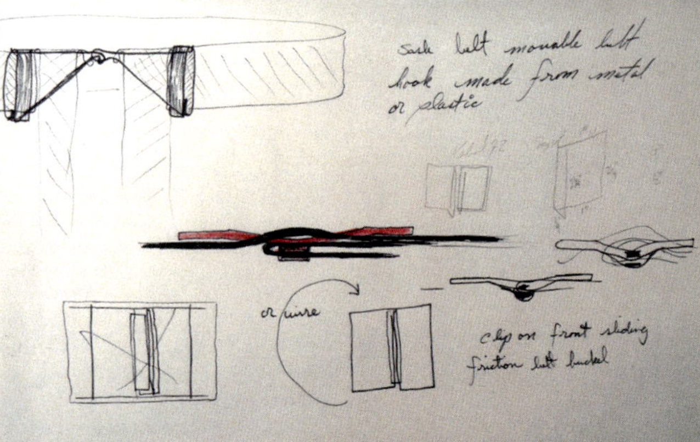

76:15 They shall be served with silver dishes, and beakers as large as goblets which they themselves shall measure: and cups brim-full with ginger-flavored water from the Fount of Selsabil. They shall be attended by boys graced with eternal youth, who to the beholder's eyes will seem like sprinkled pearls. when you gaze upon that scene you will behold a kingdom blissful and glorious.

76:28 The unbelievers love this fleeting life too well, and thus prepare for themselves a heavy day of doom. We created them, and endowed their limbs and joints with strength: but if We please We can replace them by other men.

98: The Proof

98:1 The unbelievers among the People of the Book [Jews and Christians] and the pagans did not desist from unbelief until the Proof was given them: an apostle from Allah reading sanctified pages from eternal scriptures.

* *The Koran* -- a few talking points

I enjoy studying diverse value systems as I try to sort through that which holds human affection generation after generation. Having put together successful merchant adventures in California, New York, London, Paris, Geneva, Beirut, Tokyo, and Beijing, I have come to appreciate that there is only one GOLD appearing in diverse forms, while there remains disagreement over the existence of GOD in any form. ...There is dogmatic consistency in these dynamics which impact how people invest their money. Navigation is the key. Clearly, making sense of these factors is THE most ancient maze game, one that defined and defines day and night along the Silk Road.

I created this quick look at my paperback Koran as food for thought for my mother, an American rust-belt Christian who believed in the righteousness of Manifest Destiny and held all non-Christians in smug disdain. One might regard her as a bigot, however, I set aside her God/mother/country hurl, and saw her as simply cursed with a dangerous taste for decorated Christmas cookies, jellybean-filled Easter eggs, and Halloween candy corn. What else can you do?

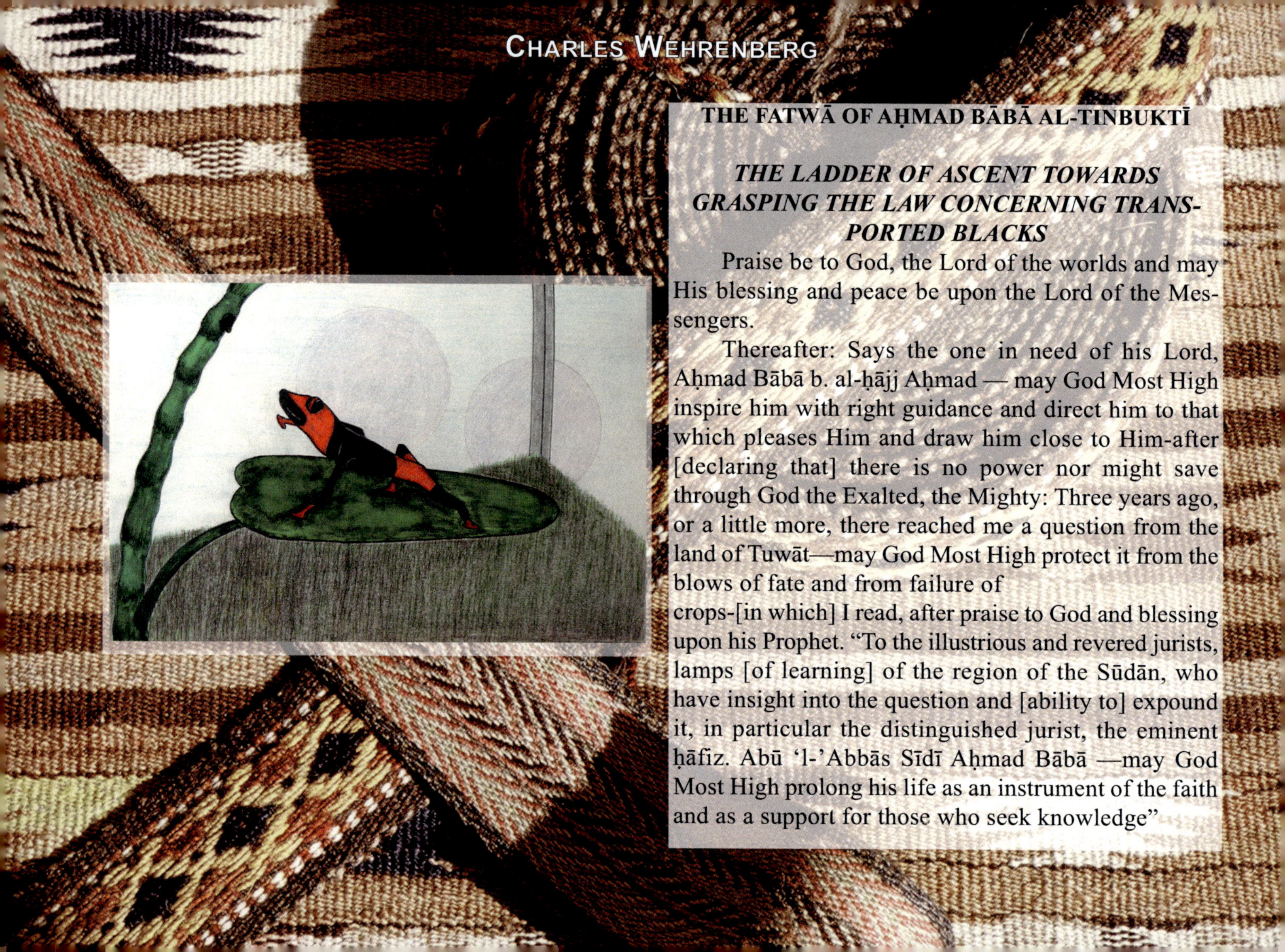

THE FATWĀ OF AḤMAD BĀBĀ AL-TINBUKTĪ

THE LADDER OF ASCENT TOWARDS GRASPING THE LAW CONCERNING TRANSPORTED BLACKS

Praise be to God, the Lord of the worlds and may His blessing and peace be upon the Lord of the Messengers.

Thereafter: Says the one in need of his Lord, Aḥmad Bābā b. al-ḥājj Aḥmad — may God Most High inspire him with right guidance and direct him to that which pleases Him and draw him close to Him-after [declaring that] there is no power nor might save through God the Exalted, the Mighty: Three years ago, or a little more, there reached me a question from the land of Tuwāt—may God Most High protect it from the blows of fate and from failure of crops-[in which] I read, after praise to God and blessing upon his Prophet. "To the illustrious and revered jurists, lamps [of learning] of the region of the Sūdān, who have insight into the question and [ability to] expound it, in particular the distinguished jurist, the eminent ḥāfiz. Abū 'l-'Abbās Sīdī Aḥmad Bābā —may God Most High prolong his life as an instrument of the faith and as a support for those who seek knowledge"

Now I had the intention of writing about the matter at the time, but something prevented me from so doing until it passed into the category of things forgotten. And now there arrived at the end of this year, that is 1023/1614-15, a request for a reply to it.

Be aware, sir, that I am not, by God, a jurist, nor am I illustrious, neither do I deserve to be so described, either in reality or in metaphor. This is my reality and a description of my true self:

By the life of thy father, al-Mu'allā is not to be considered generous whilst any generous person exists.

But when lands are dried up and their herbage withered. dry stalks are pastured on.

I have a name, but there is no substance behind it, so if you are wise. do not be deceived by my name.

You are not the first person whom a moon deceived, nor [the first] scout for pasture allured by the verdure of a dung heap.

So let us offer the funeral prayer for the disappearance of learning and its practitioners, the blotting out of its sun, the eclipse of its moon. and its evanescence, as was promised by the Truthful One, may God bless him and grant him peace.

You asked: "What have you to say concerning slaves imported from lands whose people have been established to be Muslims, such as Bornu,'Afnu, Kano, Gao and Katsina, and others among whose adherence to Islam is widely acknowledged? Is it permissible to own them or not?" [The Reply]: Be it known—may God Most High grant us and you success-that the people of these lands are, as you have said, Muslims, except for 'Afnu whose location I do not know, nor have I heard of it. However, close to each of these is a land in which there are unbelievers (kafara) whom the Muslim people of these lands make raids on. Some of them, as is well known, are under their protection and pay kharāj according to what has come to our

ears. Sometimes he sultans of these lands are in a state of discord the one with the other, and the sultan of one land attacks the other and takes whatever captives he can, they being Muslims. These captives, free Muslims. are then sold-to God we belong and to Him shall we return! This is commonplace among them in their lands.

The people of Katsina attack Kano. and others do likewise. though they speak one tongue and their languages are united and their way of life similar. The only thing that distinguishes them is that some are born Muslims and others are born unbelievers. This is what confuses the situation concerning those who are brought to them, so that they do not know the true situation of the one imported".

You said: "It is known that according to the sharī'a the sole reason for being owned is unbelief (kufr). Thus whoever purchases an unbeliever is allowed to own him. In the contrary case he is not. Conversion to Islam subsequent to the existence of the aforementioned condition has no effect on continued ownership". The Reply is that this is so, provided he is not one with whom a pact has been made, or who possesses [a contract of] protection (dhimma). There is no way round that.

You asked: "Were these aforementioned lands belonging to the Muslims of the Sūdān conquered and their people enslaved in a state of unbelief, while their conversion to Islam occurred subsequently, so there is no harm [in owning them]. or not? The Reply is that they converted to Islam without anyone conquering them. like the people of Kano, Katsina. Bornu and Songhay. We never heard that anyone conquered them before their conversion to Islam. Among them are some who have long been Muslims. like the people of Bornu and Songhay.

You said: "One of the qāḍīs of the Sūdān reported that the imam who conquered them whilst they were unbelievers chose to spare them [as slaves]" I say: "This is something we have never heard of, nor has [any information about] it reached us. So ask this sūdāni qāḍī who this imam was, and at what time he conquered their land, and which land he conquered? Let him specify all of this to you. His statement is very close to being devoid of truth. If you investigate now, you will not find anyone who will confirm the truth of what he said. What is based upon what he says, therefore, is not to be given consideration. God Most High knows best. Look at the statement of Walī 'l-Din Ibn Khaldūn concerning the people of Bornu, which will be given later, if God Most High wills. You asked if this is correct or not. The reply is that in all probability it is incorrect.

You asked: "How could this be so in regard to the people of Bornu, which is the abode of their sultanate, and people are frequently brought to us from there. Are they slaves or not?" Reply is that they are free Muslims, who converted to Islam long ago. However, close to their borders are unbelievers whom they raid and take hold of and sell, as we have said before. In the "Great History" of the imam, the ḥāfiz Walī 'l-Din Ibn Khaldūn, when he gave an account of the Ḥafṣid state in Tunis, is the statement: "In the year 55—that is 655 [1257-8]—there arrived in Tunis a gift from the king of Kanem, who is the ruler of Bornu [which lies] south of Tripoli. Part of it consisted of a giraffe, a creature of strange form, of contradictory traits and appearance. It was a huge attraction in Tunis. etc., etc."

Before that, when speaking of the kings of the Sūdān neighboring the Maghrib he said: "Among the peoples of the Sūdān are the Tājura and they are bordered by the Kanem who are a multitudinous folk among whom Islam predominates. They hold sway over the lands of the Sahara up to Fezzan. They engaged in an exchange of gifts with the Ḥafṣid state from its inception. They are bordered in the west by Kawkaw and after them Wanghāra and al-Takrūr" and later he said: "When Ifrīqiyya was conquered, the merchants entered the lands of the west, and found among them none more mighty than the king of Ghāna [whose people] border the Encompassing Ocean on the western side. They were the mightiest nation (umma) and had the largest kingdom. The seat of their king [was] Ghāna, two towns on the banks of the Nile, one of the mightiest and most populous cities in the world. The author of the Kitāb Rūjār mentioned it, as did the author of al-Masālik wa'l-mamālik. On the eastern side their neighbors were another nation called Ṣuṣu, spelled with two ṣāds each with a damma. Then after it is another nation known as Mālī. Then after it another nation known as Kawkaw", down to where he said, "Then the dominion of the people of Ghāna weakened and dwindled while the veiled ones (al-mulaththimūn) to their north adjoining the lands of the Berbers grew powerful, as we have already said, and lorded it over the Sūdān, plundered their heartlands and their territories and exacted tribute and jizya. They forced many of them into Islam, which they adopted as a religion. Then the authority of the rulers of Ghāna diminished and they were conquered by the Ṣuṣu people, one of the nations of the Sūdān, who enslaved them and assimilated them to their number. Then the people of Mālī became the largest of the nations of the Sūdān in these regions of theirs and grew powerful, so they conquered the ~u~u", until he said, "and they were Muslims", [and so on] down to the end of what he said.

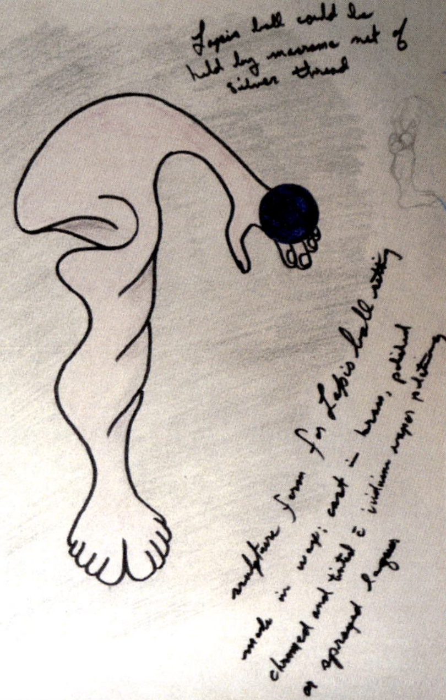

You said: "Was their land taken by force or by agreement?" The Reply is that what is apparent from what Ibn Khaldūn and others said is that they became Muslims of their own free will".

You said: "Similarly he

whose land [of origin] is unknown and whose status is unclear, and it is not known whether his enslavement preceded his conversion to Islam or not: is it permissible to buy him and sell him without investigation? Or is investigation mandatory, or is it [merely] recommended?" The Reply is that you know that the cause of enslavement is unbelief, and the unbelievers of the Sūdān are like any other unbelievers in this regard- Jews, Christians, Persians, Berbers or others whose persistence in unbelief rather than Islam has been established-as will emerge from the words of the Mudawwana at the end of this section. This is proof that there is no difference between any unbelievers in this regard. Whoever is enslaved in a state of unbelief may rightly be owned, whoever he is, as opposed to those of all groups who converted to Islam of their own free will, such as the people of Bornu, Kano, Songhay, Katsina, Gobir and Mālī and some of [the people of] Zakzak. They are free Muslims who may not be enslaved under any circumstance. So also are the majority of the Fulani, except, so we have heard, a group living beyond Jenne who are said to be unbelievers. We do not know if [their unbelief] is ancestral or occurred through apostasy. Indeed. disputes occur between them and they raid one another.

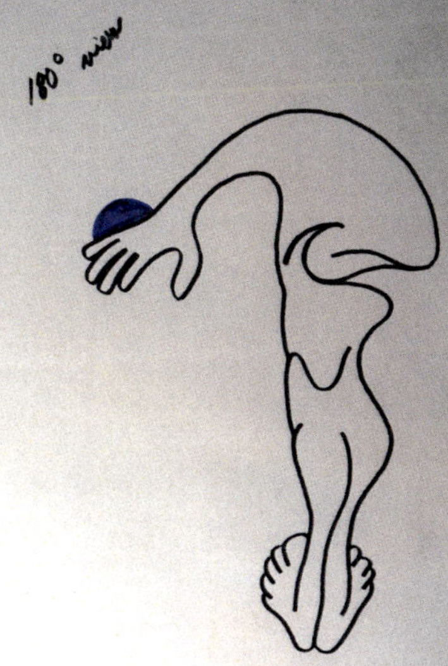

In the Nawāzil of Abū 'l-Asbagh ['Īsā] b. Sahl [we read]: "The generally accepted view (al-mash'hūr) is that whoever claims to be free and mentions that he is from a land in which free persons are frequently sold, and if the purchaser confirms that he bought him from such a land, then, according to Muhammad b. al-Walīd and Yaḥāy b. 'Abd al-'Aziz, the purchaser is charged with proving the person's slave status. Saḥnūn said: 'And Ibn Lubābā said: "The one who claims he is free must provide the proof. Abū 'All used to rule in accordance with what our colleagues said, because of the wickedness of the times, but I do not hold such a view'". Ibn Zurb said: It is up to the owner to prove the validity of his purchase from the former owner. The ruled in accordance with this during the rebellion of Ibn Ḥafṣūn"'. End [of quotation]. [Saḥnūn] mentioned this in juridical problems relating to manumission, before [the section on] marriages. He mentioned many details

relating to this and replies to them which would be tedious to quote here, so they may be consulted there.

Our master the jurist, the blessing, the exemplar, Mahmūd b. Umar b. Muhammad Aqīt used to give judgment in his time in favor of the claimant of free status and remove him from the control of whoever he was with until [lawful] ownership was established, in accordance with what the aforementioned group [of jurists] ruled. If it was not, then he ruled to declare him free. The ḥāfiz Makhlūf al-Balbālī also gave a fatwā saying: "Slavery is rooted in unbelief. The unbelievers of the Sūdān are like the Christians, except that they are Majūs. The Muslims among them, like the people of Kano, Katsina, Bornu, Gobir and all of Songhay, are Muslims whom it is not permissible to own: However, some of them attack others, raiding them unjustly, like the Arabs who attack free Muslims and sell them unjustly. None of them' may be lawfully possessed. Whoever is known to be from those lands which are known for their Islam, and states that he is from those lands, should be let go and adjudged to be free, as ruled the jurists of al-Andalus like Ibn 'Attāb and others. They were only opposed by Ibn Lubābā. The judges of Fez ruled in like manner as did Sīdī Mahmūd qāḍī of Timbuktu. He would accept their word without requiring them to prove that they were from those lands. Whoever seeks salvation for himself should not purchase any of them except [in cases where] some one names his land and it is investigated whether or not he is from that land, that is to say from a land of Islam or a land of unbelievers. This is a great calamity whose misfortune has become widespread in this age and in these lands". Here ends the quotation of the Shaykh Makhlūf in abridged form as I found it copied from him. I say: "The reply to your question as to whether the slave's word is to be accepted or not is apparent from this".

You said: "[An opinion] was given in one of the replies of the Jurist, the ḥāfiz- Abū Isḥāq Ibrāhīm b. Hilāl that refraining from becoming owners of them in cases of doubt comes under the heading of [religious] scrupulousness. This view it would seem -God knows best-is based on the statement of Ibn Lubābā: 'because [the slave] is in his possession and [the owner] has power over him'. And he was of the view that letting such a person go and not having ownership of him comes under the heading of [religious] scrupulousness in keeping with the view of the body of jurists (al-jamā'a). God knows best". You asked: "Does this come under the heading of doubt about the impediment and should [ownership] therefore be nullified-as in the case of doubt in divorce-or has it to do with doubt about the condition, necessitating the pre-existence of that which is subject to the condition, as is the case in doubt over ritual impurity". The Reply is that the question comes under the heading of doubt about the cause, so it would seem, since the cause for possession is unbelief, so ponder this. God knows best.

You said: "Is it established that the Prophet—may God bless him and grant him peace-and his Companions used to make investigations in this sense when they wanted to acquire possession [of a slave]. The Reply is that the circumstances of people in his day—

may God bless him and grant him peace-and that of his Companions—may God's good pleasure be upon them-were well-known because of the predominance of unbelief among people in those days. Hence the circumstance of whatever slave was acquired in those days was known because he was one of the unbelievers, since those who had converted to Islam in those days were also known. At that time the Ḥabasha were unbelievers except for those who had converted to Islam like the Najāshī, I mean Aṣḥama, and a few others of his people. Upon his death they continued as unbelievers at the time, so it was proper to possess those of them

who had [already] been possessed, since their owners were certain of their circumstance and of their unbelief. There is no interpretation that permits their being possessed-either they or any others except unbelief-since the apostate can neither be confirmed in his unbelief nor can he be possessed.

As regards the ḥadīth which you cited from Jalāl al-Dīn al-Suyūṭī's Azhār al-urūsh fi akhbār al-Ḥubūsh, coming from the ḥadīth of al-Hākim on the authority of Ibn Mas'ūd, that Noah was bathing and saw his son looking at him and said to him, "Are you watching me bathe? May God change your color!" And he became black and he is the ancestor of the sudān-I came across it myself in his book entitled Raf' sha'n al-Ḥubshān, and the actual words are: "As for the blackness of their skins, Ibn al-Jawzi said: 'It is evident that they were created as they are without any apparent reason'. However, we narrate [the following account]: 'The children of Noah divided up the earth and the children of Shem settled at the center of the earth and they had amongst them both darkness of skin and whiteness. The sons of Japheth settled in a northerly and in an easterly direction and they had amongst them both redness and blondness. The sons of Ham settled in the south and in the west and their colors changed'. He [Ibn al-Jawzi] said: 'As for what is related about Noah's nakedness being exposed and Ham not covering it and being cursed, this is something not proven and is not correct'".

Al-Jalāl al-Suyūṭī said: "I say: This is supported by what Umm al-Faḍl informed me of through [my] study [with her] (qirā ʻatan) [saying] Abū Isḥāq al-Tha'ālibī told us [saying] Abū 'l-Ḥasan al-Dāwudī told us [saying] Abū Muhammad al-Sarakhsī told us [saying] Abū Isḥāq al-Shāsi told us [saying] 'Abd Allāh b. Humayd told us [saying] Hud b. Khalifa told us [saying] 'Awf b. Qasāma told us on the authority of Zuhayr who said: "I heard al-Ash'arī say: 'The Messenger of God—may God bless him and grant him peace—said: "Ādam was created from a handful [of earth] which [God] took from all parts of the world. Hence his offspring turned out according to the earth [they were made from]; some came out red. others white, others black, some were easy-going, others downcast, some were evil and others good'. This is a sound ḥadīth published by al-Ḥākim in al-Mustadrak, and it is to be relied upon in [the matter of] the blackness of their color, for it is a reversion to the clay from which they were created. As for what Ibn al-Jawzi denied, Ibn Jarir [al-Ṭabarī] published it in his History. He said: 'Salama told us on the authority of Ibn Isḥāq who said: "The people of the Torah claim that this only came about through a curse uttered by Noah against Ham. It happened that Noah slept and his nakedness was uncovered, and Ham saw it and did not cover it up. Shem and Japheth saw it and cast a cloth upon it and covered up hisnakedness. When he awoke he realized what Ham had done and what Shem and Japheth had done and he made mention of it. Amongst what he said was: 'He', that is Shem, 'is blessed and Ham shall be a slave to his two brothers"'. Ibn Jadr continued: 'Others than Ibn Isḥāq said that Noah prayed that the prophets and mes-

sengers should come from Shem's progeny, and he prayed that kings should come from Japhet's descendants, and he cursed Ham saying that his color should be changed and his descendants should be slaves of the descendants of Shem and Japheth'". End of quotation [from Raf sha'n al-Ḥubshān].

And your statement concerning the name of the book Azhār al-urūsh, I came across it in the land of Dar'a, but I am now uncertain whether it was the book itself or the abridgment of it Nūr al-ghabash fi akhbār al-Ḥabash. I say: Likewise the Imam, the most mindful ḥāfiz Ibn Khaldūn said in his history entitled Kitāb al'ibar wa-dīwān al-mubtada' wa'l-khabar fi akhbār al-'Arab wa'l-Ajam wa 'l-Barbar as follows: "As for those climes that are distant from the median (al-i'tidāl) like the first and second and the sixth and seventh", [and so on] until he said, "Some genealogists who have no knowledge of the way in which the world works (tabā'i' al-kā'ināt) imagined that the sūdān are the children of Noah's son Ham, who were distinguished by blackness of skin color on account of a curse from his father, the effect of which appeared in their color, and the slavery which God assigned to his descendants. Noah's curse is [mentioned] in the Torah, but there is no mention there of blackness. He merely cursed him [praying that] his children should be slaves to the children of his brothers, nothing more. Attributing blackness to Ham on this account is to ignore the nature of heat and cold and their effect on the atmosphere and the creatures that have their existence within it, namely the universality of blackness among the people of the first and second climes due to their climate being affected by a double heat in the south, for the sun is directly over their heads twice every year in quick succession. Hence direct overhead sun persists in most seasons, and thus the light is intense and extreme heat beats down on them and their skins are blackened from the excessive heat. Opposite to these two climes in the north are the sixth and seventh climes whose inhabitants are universally white due to their climate being subject to extreme cold in the north. since the sun is continuously on the horizon, or almost so, wherever the eye looks in the circle of vision, and it does not rise to

the zenith or even come close to it. Hence the heat there is weak, and coldness extends over most seasons, and people become white in color, ending up bleached. This in turn leads to what inevitably results from exposure to an extremely cold climate, namely blue eyes, blotched skins, and reddish hair. Have a look at the rest of it, for it is lengthy. This was what Ibn Sīnā was referring to in his rajaz verses on medicine when he said:

The Zanj have heat which changes their bodies, till it clothed their skins in blackness.

The Slavs have acquired a whiteness so that their skins became gleaming.

You asked: "What is the meaning of Ham's children being slaves to the children of Japheth and Shem? If he meant the unbelievers, then this is not a peculiarity of theirs. On the contrary, it is so in regard to the children of his brothers Japheth and Shem since unbelief allows their being possessed [as slaves], whether they are black or white". The Reply is that the legal position is like that. This is not a peculiarity of theirs. Indeed, any unbeliever among the children of Ham or anyone else may be possessed [as a slave] if he remains attached to his original unbelief. There is no difference between one race and another. Perhaps it was that his curse was effective on most of them, not all of them. In the Hadīth [we read]: "I prayed my Lord not to destroy my community by drought, and he granted me that [etc.], down to where he said: "I called on my Lord not to let troubles occur amongst them, and he denied me that", etc. As for the ḥadīth: "Look after the sūdān, for among them are three of the lords of Paradise", there

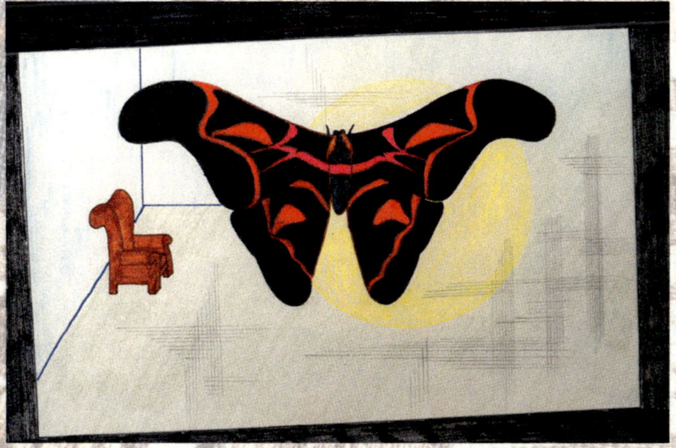

is a command in it to look after them, so that people would not dislike them on account of some of their objectionable characteristics, and their general lack of refinement. The Prophet only gave such a command-though God alone knows best-and encouraged people to observe it because of the rapidity with which the sūdān are subdued and become obedient and are driven in whichever direction they are led, and the speed with which they embrace Islam, so that there might well be among them lords like those elect Muslims or similarly others of their lords. Al-Jalāl al-Suyūṭī enumerated many of them in his book Raj sha'n

al-Hubshan.

As for the ḥadīth: "Your brothers are your slaves", it contains an admonition to be kind and compassionate to him among them who is owned, as well as others. and to treat him kindly and compassionately, since the mere fact of being owned generally breaks one's heart, because dominance and subordination associated with this condition. especially when one is far from home. [As the poet said] "The stranger who is decked out in finery is [nevertheless]
regarded with disdain".

For all men are the sons of Adam. Hence [the Prophet] said: "God caused you to own him, and had He wished. He would have caused him to own you", or words to that effect, to make you aware of the fact that He made his favor to you complete through Islam and that He afflicted the slave, or his forebears, with unbelief up to [the time when] he was captured. God knows best.

You said concerning the ḥadīth "God put them under your authority": (Does this concern[only] him whose slave status was concomitant with his unbelief or is this not specified, and in such a case what does this mean'?'. The answer is that [the Prophet]—may God bless him and grant him peace-said it—God knows best concerning him who is possessed on account of unbelief, which is what gives rise to being possessed. whether or not he converted to Islam subsequently or continued in his unbelief. Reflect on the case of Abū Lu'lu'a—may God Most High Curse him-the slave of al-Mugīra b. Shu'ba. who killed

'Umar b. al-Khaṭṭāb, may God be pleased with him. Abū Lu'lu'a complained to 'Umar about the heaviness of his indemnity, so 'Umar, may God be pleased with him, ordered him to pay what he thought he could bear, and he intended at the same time to tell al-Mughīra to lighten his indemnity.

But the wretched outcast was not able to wait patiently for him to tell him, since he had been suffering for a long time, so he assassinated him in dastardly fashion, as is reported in the Ṣaḥīḥ.

You state: "It is established that during the days of the Prophet—may God bless him and grant him peace—the Ḥabash accepted to Islam, and that the Prophet—may God bless him and grant him peace—and his Companions owned many of them, as has already been said. Did they hesitate over owning them, or did they do so without caring?"

The Reply, as we stated before, is that the circumstance of the Ḥabash was well-known to them, and that he among them or among others v:ho was possessed had not abandoned his unbelief at the time (If his capture, and that the one among them who converted to Islam was the Najāshī, that is Aṣḥama, while they [the other Ḥabash] continued in their unbelief. The imam Ibn Khaldūn said in his history when speaking of the different types of sūdān in the fourth volume: "Ḥabasha is the mightiest nation of the Blacks. They neighbor the Yemen on the western shore of the [Red] Sea. They were Christians and then one of them converted to Islam at the time of the hijra, according to what is established in the Sahīh. Then they returned to their reli-

gion. The one who converted to Islam at the time of the Prophet—may God bless him and grant him peace-and to whom the Companions made hijra before the hijra to Medina, and who sheltered them and protected them, and who was prayed for by the Prophet—may God bless him and grant him peace when his death was announced to him, was called al-Najāshī'. Later he said: "To the west of it is the town of Dāmūr where there is one of the mightiest of kings who has a huge kingdom.(" To its north is another king called Haqq al-Din Muhammad b. 'Ali b. Walaṣma 'in the town of Wāfāt. His forebears converted to Islam at an unknown date.

His grandfather Walaṣma' was subject to the king of Dāmūr. Al-Khaṭṭī was seized by jealousy because of this and attacked him and took possession of his land. Then civil war broke out and the authority of al-Khaṭṭī weakened. The sons of Walaṣma' took back their land and seized Wāfāt which they laid waste. We have heard that Ḥaqq al-Din perished and that he was succeeded by his brother Sa'd al-Din. They are Muslims and are subject sometimes to al-Khaṭṭī, whilst at others they resist him. God is the Possessor of Sovereignty". End of quotation

Your statement: "Is the ruling concerning imported ḥabash the same as the ruling concerning imported sūdān. or is there a difference?

The Reply is as we stated previously, that is that there is no difference between any unbelievers, except for those with whom a pact has been made and the Protected Persons and apostates, as regards raiding them and having free rein to possess those captured-sūdān, Christians, Jews and others being alike in this.

In the Mudawwana in the first book on zakāt [we read]: "Jizya is to be taken from him who professes a religion other than Islam: and it is not to be doubled for the Christians of Banu Taghlib or for others·" And at the end of the book on zakāt in the Mudawwana in the chapter on taking jizya from the Majūs, the Berbers, the Fezzanis, the Sicilians and others of the non-Arabs, is the following statement: "The Prophet, may God bless him and grant him peace, saId: 'Treat them like the People of the Scripture', and 'Uthmān took jizya from the majūs of the Berbers. Mālik said: 'All non-Arab peoples who have no scripture, whether Fezzanis, Slavs, Berbers, Turks or others, have the status of majūs in this matter. If they are summoned to Islam and do not respond [favorably], they are to be summoned to payment of jizya and left to profess their religions. If they respond [favorably], the response is to be accepted"'. End of verbatim quotation.

Your statement: "Also the dictum of the jurists [that] slavery is a mark of unbelief. What does this mean?" The Reply is that the cause of slavery is unbelief. Any slave who is possessed is a proof of having been taken captive, either him or his forebear. God Most High knows best.

Your statement: "Be so kind as to remove the veil from the various aspects of the problem, and satisfy our desire by giving a detailed reply for we have not found anyone who gives full satisfaction in all aspects of that matter, except for what comes from your direction, with the help of God Most High, though committing an error in the matter is a grave danger. All lands and regions are generally afflicted by it, so haply may God provide illumination in its regard at your hand. [God]-Sublime is He—is the one from whom it is asked that your reward be doubled and your treasure made abundant.

I say: "We have pursued the matter in as far as it was possible for us and to the extent of God's blessing. What is correct came through God's bounty and in His praise. What is error came from its own place and from its author.

We will add another rule for you, that is that whoever now comes to you from the group called Mossi, or Gurma, or Busa, or Borgu, or Dagomba, or Kotokoli, or Yoruba, or Tombo, or Bobo, or K.rmu—all of these are unbelievers, remaining in their unbelief until now. Similarly Kumbe, except for a few of the people of Hombori and Da'nakā, though their Islam is shallow, so there is no harm in possessing them

without posing questions. This is the rule regarding these groups. God Most High knows best and is the Best Judge.

Let this be the end of what we attempt in "The Ladder of Ascent towards grasping the Law concerning Transported Black Africans", or If you wish call it "The Exposition and Explanation concerning the Varieties of Transported Black Africans". May God seal you and us with faith and make us among the folk of goodliness, through the grace of the lord of the progeny of 'Adnān —may God bless him and his Family and his Companions, so long as day follows night, and so long as man finds joy in achieving his desire. Our last prayer is that praise be to God the Lord of the Worlds, and may God bless our master Muhammad, His Prophet, and grant him peace, likewise all those who follow him in goodliness to the Day of Judgment.

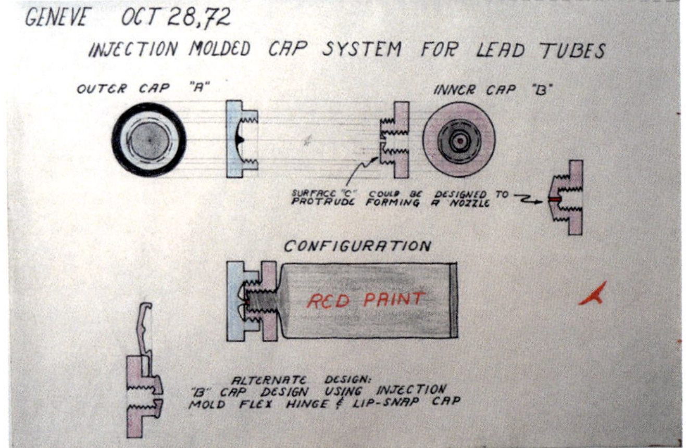

Dated Monday 10 Muḥarram 1024/9 February 1615, at the hand of its compiler Aḥmad Bābā b. Aḥmad b. Aḥmad b. 'Umar b.Muḥammad Aqīt—may God inspire in him right guidance.

THE QUESTIONS OF AL-ĪSĪ
AND THE REPLIES OF AḤMAD BĀbĀ
THE FIRST QUESTION

In the name of God the Compassionate, the Merciful. And may God bless our lord and master Muhammad and his Family

May God preserve you Sayyid Aḥmad Bābā b. Aḥmad and watch over you. Peace be upon you and the mercy of God and His blessings. Your answer, master of ours, about the slaves of your area, the land of the Sūdān, as regards those whom it was permissible to buy and sell and to possess, in your land, in past times and what has been customary in your lands, considering that there are [many] jurists and imams of the faith among you. Sīdī Makhlūf al-Balbālī mentioned in his reply that those among them who are Muslims, like the people of Kano and some of Zakzak and the people of Katsina and the people of Gobir and all of Songhay-all of them are Muslims and it is not lawful to own them. Similarly all of the Fulani, though they dispute with one another and some raid others and some sell others, making predatory incursions, unjustly and aggressively, like the Arabs who attack free Muslims and sell them unjustly. It is not lawful to possess any of them. End of what we want [to quote] from his reply—may God have mercy on him.

Then we wish you to give clarification of this question, since Islam may have entered some of these lands after his death, or [in other cases] it may have disappeared, and [people] may have returned to unbelief. We also wish to have your reply about what we shall mention concerning what we heard about the names of some tribes, and what you know about the lands and tribes we have not heard of. Among those whom we heard were Muslims are: S.n.w.r, Gashgashī, Gao, Katsina, Gobir, Zawzaw, Bornu, Kabi and Kulani. Sīdī Makhlūf did not mention these among those whom he designated as Muslims. Perhaps the difference lies in the names being too specific or too general.

Among those whom we heard were unbelievers are: Gurma, Borgu, Irbā (Yoruba), Dagomba. Kurwā, Tondinke, Kotokoli, G.n.b.sh and Mossi.

Those are what my mind could grasp as far as what we heard about lands of Islam and lands of unbelief are concerned. Perhaps there are other lands and tribes of either type whom we have not heard of.

Similarly these Sīwī Arabs who come to our lands as slaves (bi'l-milkiyya) and some Sanhāja from the province and area of the Sūdān. Explain their case to us. Are they followers of Islam or unbelievers, or are there both types among them at the same time? Explain to us the two types whom Sīdī Makhlūf mentioned were partly Muslim, though he did not specify [who were] the Muslims or the unbelievers, so that we could discover the truth regardmg all who are lawful to be owned and those who are to be avoided. Likewise Jolof and Jenne. May God aid you and prolong your existence. Amen

THE FIRST REPLY

Praise be to God Alone. May God bless Muhammad and his Family and grant them peace.

May God preserve you, Sire, and cause you and us to prosper, and count us among those who are scrupulous about areas of doubt and make us beware of the pitfalls of perdition. Peace bc upon you and the mercy of God.

What I think regarding your question is that you ought to know first that some of these groups (aṣnāf) are mixed together. Those whom we have ascertained to be Muslim are all of the people of Songhay and its kingdom [stretching for a distance of] some two months in length. Similarly all of Kano are Muslims since ancient times, likewise Katsina and Zakzak and Gobir. However, close to them are unbelieving people whom the Muslims may raid because of their extreme proximity, so we have heard. and they bring them to their place as unbelievers and slaves. As regards these people, if it is established among you that a slave woman or man is from these unbelievers and was merely raised in the city of Kano or Katsina or Zakzak or Kabi, and subsequently converted to Islam, then there is no harm in buying him, since he was taken captive while an unbeliever.

Similarly, all the people of Bornu are Muslims, but close to them also are unbelievers whom the people of Bornu raid. The ruling is as before.

As for Tondike this is a name applied to those who live in the Land of the Rock, since tondi means 'rock' in our language, and the kāf is for the nisba, as is also the yā in our language also. The People of the Rock are of different groups: some are Muslims, people of Tawḥīd, such as the people of Hombori and Da'nankā

and Gili. These are free Muslims. If anyone of them is made captive,
then beware and keep clear of him, for he is a free Muslim. Then there are the people of Dum and the people of Armina and Kiray and Kuru, forming part of another populace which only their Creator can count. These groups are unbelievers until the present day. Whomever of them you get hold of, buy him, for he was made captive as an unbeliever.

All of these are close to the sultan of Songhay. Some of them, such as the people of Arbinda and the people of Armina pay jizya. As for Gurma and Mossi and Borgu and Yoruba and Dagomba and Kotokoli, they are all unbelievers until the present time and their legal status is clear, As for Kurwā which was mentioned in your question, I do not know any group of this name in these parts. Neither do I know Kanbashi.

As for Kabi, they are a group between Songhay and Hausaland. They are now Muslims and have been for more than sixty years. As for Kulan(i), I know that this is the name of one of the territories of Songhay some ten days [travel] distant from Gao. Its people are Muslims. Similarly the people of Jenne. They are among the choicest of God's servants in their Islam. Before the present day they had among them great jurisprudents and scholars and pious men who were counted among the Friends of God and those [blessed with] karāmāt. In sum, down to the present day they are fine people, religious and goodly, extremely generous and full of affection and kindness towards the stranger. It is said to have been proven that goodness and kindness are in its water, and whoever reaches the town and drinks its water feels in himself something he has never before experienced.

As for Bambara and Bobo, they are groups of unbelievers living beyond Jenne until the present time, and they are unbelievers. As for Jolof, its people are, according to what we have heard, and indeed what has been confirmed, Muslims, among whom are scholars (talaba), Ṣūfis (fuqarā') and memorizers of the kor'ān. As for Fulani, they are also Muslims. However, the behaviour of some of them is not pleasing, since evil conduct, raiding and predatoriness predominate among them. Nevertheless, that does not deny them the name of Muslims.

As for Gashgashi, this is a name I have never

heard of except in this land of yours. What I understood from it is that it is a name applied to the people of Hausa. If this is so, then they are the prementioned groups, the people of Katsina, Kabi, Zakzak, Bornu, Kano and Gobir. As has previously been said, they are Muslims, and near them are a group of unbelievers, such as the people of Zamfara and others.

This is the reply it has been possible to write—may God Most High preserve us from all trials and tribulations and save us on the Day of Gathering and Dispersal. The humble servant of God, the one in need [of God] Aḥmad Bābā b. Ahmad b. al-hājj Aḥmad — may God show beneficence to them all—Amen, writes [this], greeting you with peace.

It is important to inform you also about the Bulāla people. They are folk who are mixed, having among them Arabs, Fulani, and sūdān. As for the people of Sīwā, they are Arabs who claim that to be from Judhām, and the Judhām, as is known, are from Saba'.Until today they speak: Classical Arabic and their situation is like that of the Arabs, though it is said that many of them do not belong to the [Muslim] community (milla). Hence the scholars of Kano disagreed over whether they could be enslaved or not. One of them gave a judicial opinion that they could be enslaved, saying that they were unbelievers and their conversion to Islam had not been established, and that their claim to be Arabs was [a mere] assertion. Another gave the opinion that it was not permissible to enslave them. I contend that his fatwā is weak, for even if people are to be believed concerning their genealogies, as Mālīk said, nevertheless, it is authoritatively established that among the Arabs there are some who did not convert to Islam. and that Arabs may be enslaved, with the exception of Quraysh. If such folk are now described as unbelievers, what should be understood is that either they are currently unbelievers, or that their ancestors were apostates. This is how it seemed to me formerly when we were asked about it when we were in Timbuktu.

As for the Bulāla people, they are Muslims, I mean the Arabs and the Fulani and the sūdān. However the ruler of Bornu, the sultan called Idrīs -an unenlightened (jāhil) man, so we have heard — imposed his sovereignty upon them. May God Most High mete out justice—he guides to the [right] path. Peace. From the one who wrote it, Aḥmad Bābā—may God grant him success. Amen.

Written by him who seeks success from God, so as to put it into practice, the servant of God Most High, who hopes for the pardon of his Lord, Yusuf b. Ibrāhīm b. ʻAmr—may God support him through his grace.

The question is in the hand of him who wrote it, and the reply (was copied from) the hand of the one questioned, the jurisprudent the man of letters, the muḥaddith, the polymath Sīd(ī) Aḥmad b. Aḥmad b. 'Umar b.Muḥammad Aqīt al-Sanhājī and Masnuwī al-Takrūrī al-Tinbuktī al-Mālikī—may God preserve him.

*****

credits and access:

Publications of the Institute of African Studies

Rabat 2000

Annotated and Translated by

John O. Hunwick (1936-2015) & Fatima Karrak

text with footnotes online at:

https://www.artsrn.ualberta.ca/amcdouga/Hist347/autumn%202012/additional%20readings/ahmad_baba.pdf

also available at: https://www.jstor.org/stable/25653344

SUPER BALL
KMPX · FIRST · BIRTHDAY · BENEFIT
APRIL
THIRD ·
WEDNESDAY
6 TIL 2
WINTERLAND

Ed Bear in Kauai 1973

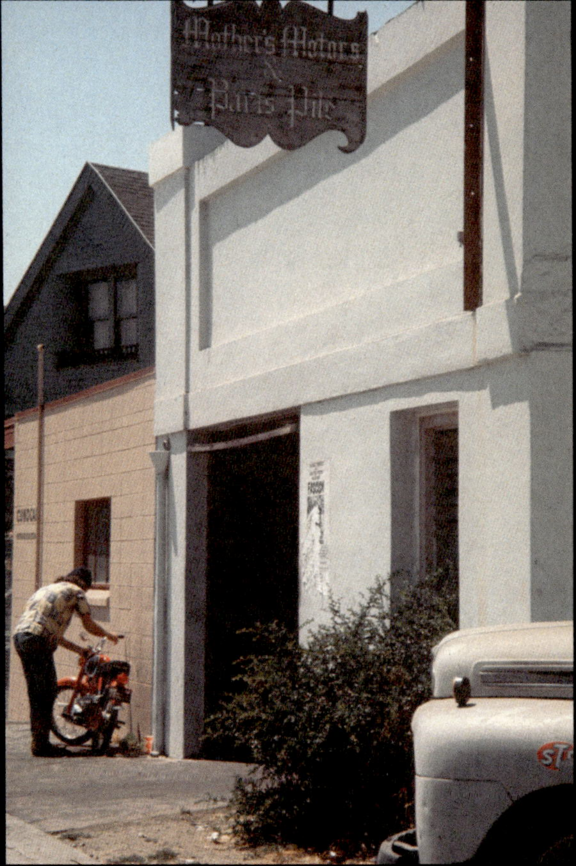
Mother's Motors
&
Parts Pile

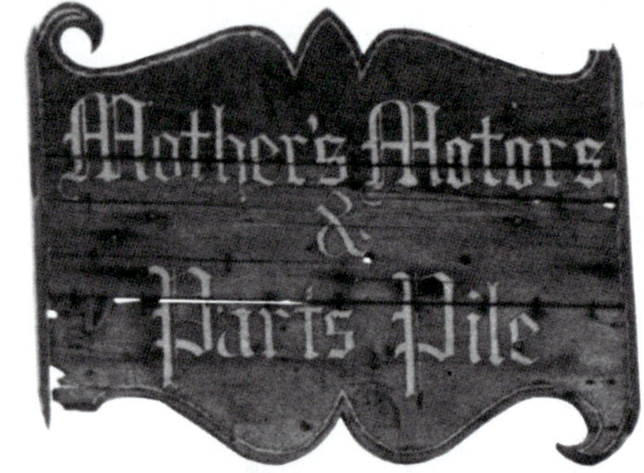

Mother's Motors
&
Parts Pile

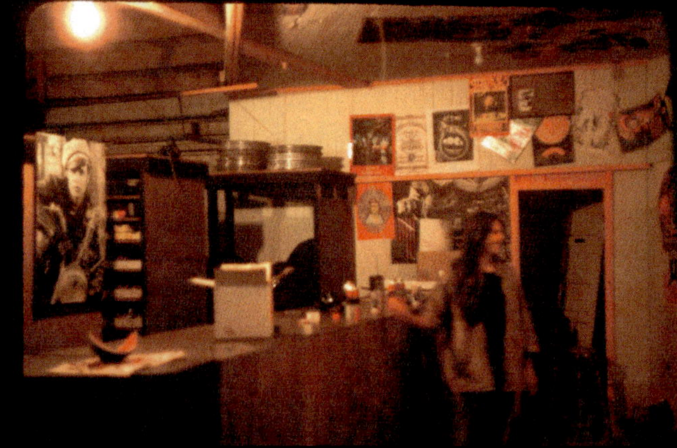

Berkeley California 1967/68

Sally Larsen

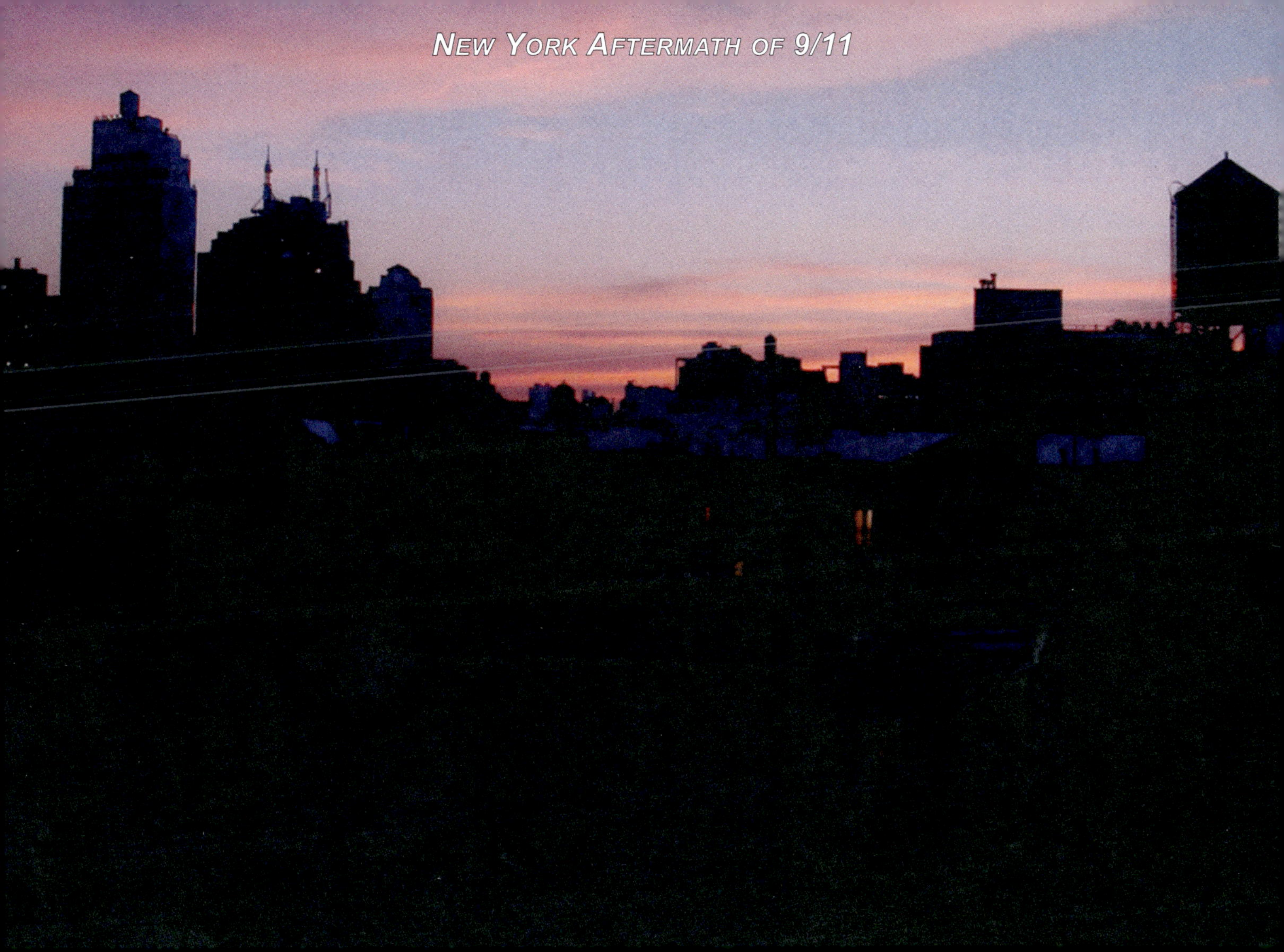

WANTED
DEAD OR
May your Death be long & Plentiful
Osama bin Laden
For mass murder in New York City

SPORTS FINAL
DAILY NEWS
NEW YORK'S HOMETOWN NEWSPAPER
48 SPECIAL
I ♥ NY
MORE THAN EVER
Milton Glaser's reinterpretation of his celebrated 1975 poster

BUILDING BRIDGES
From SYDNEY
to
NEW YORK

THESE BRAVE SOULS
JOSHUA
(212) 927-4529
LOVED ONES

AA

SZP

Made in the USA
Columbia, SC
26 June 2023